A to Z Hints for the Vegetable Gardener

Library of Congress Catalog Card Number: 75-39519

International Standard Book Number: 0-88266-106-X Paperback

Printed in United States of America

Printing (last digit): 10 9 8 7

Address all correspondence to: Men's Garden Clubs of America, 5560 Merle Hay Road, Des Moines, Iowa 50323.

In their gardens...
Bob Sanders [below]
Bob Fischer [right]

MEN'S GARDEN CLUBS OF AMERICA'S

A TO Z HINTS
FOR THE
VEGETABLE GARDENER

Compiled by

ROBERT E. SANDERS
Des Moines Chapter
Men's Garden Clubs of America

Illustrated by

ROBERT V. FISCHER
Des Moines Chapter
Men's Garden Clubs of America

Garden Way Publishing Edition

**ON BEHALF OF ITS 10,000 MEMBERS NATIONWIDE,
THE MEN'S GARDEN CLUBS OF AMERICA
PROUDLY DEDICATES THIS, ITS FIRST BOOK...**

- *TO* renowned horticulturist Harold J. Parnham, Charter Member (1932) and 1975 National President of the Men's Garden Clubs of America; and . . .

- *TO* the millions of American gardeners, young and young-at-heart, who have or will experience the joys and satisfactions of working in the beauty and wonder of God's plant kingdom and the rewards of harvesting the fruits of one's own labor;

Harold J. Parnham

- *TO* the memory of loved ones. . .and friends. . .and gardeners of generations past...who shared their enthusiasm and skills with seed and soil, and thus instilled the love of gardening and awe of nature that continues to enrich and inspire us all;

- *TO* the gardening innovators and experimentors of yesterday...and to today's plant breeders, horticulturists and others who carry on the vital work of developing the new technology of gardening;

- *TO* the gardeners of today who boldly blend the practical know-how and gardening lore of the past with imaginative new techniques to create garden magic;

- *TO* the experts of tomorrow. . .America's youth gardeners who -- with inspiration from the past and encouragement in the present -- will perpetuate the deep-rooted heritage of love for the land that has helped our country grow and prosper since its very beginning.

**MEN'S GARDEN CLUBS OF AMERICA
Founded September 26, 1932**

January 1, 1976

ACKNOWLEDGEMENTS . . . . .

A SPECIAL THANKS to the many members of the Men's Garden Clubs of America and friends who contributed their experiences and successes in gardening so that they could be shared with thousands of other gardeners through the pages of this book.

Consultant: *DR. LARRY C. GROVE,* former MGCA National Director, Iowa State Extension Horticulturist and Associate Garden Editor, *Better Homes and Gardens*

Layout and Art Direction: RICHARD W. CROLL

Photographs: PAUL S. DUNLAP, ROBERT V. FISCHER, PETER H. JANTZ, VICTOR E. MASTIN and *ROBERT E. SANDERS*

As a gardener, if you would like to contribute a tip to this guide, we'll be happy to consider it for future editions. Send tips to: Men's Garden Clubs of America, 5560 Merle Hay Road, Des Moines, Iowa 50323.

A TO Z HINTS FOR THE VEGETABLE GARDENER is not intended to be a complete guide to growing all vegetables. It is, instead, a compilation of hints, short cuts and gardening "know-how" — the type of practical information that can save you time, help you avoid mistakes and give you a lush, productive garden. More than 50 books on vegetables and hundreds of magazines were screened for the most up-to-date, helpful hints. Many of the tips are from MGCA members from across the country. Some were originally published in *The Gardener,* the national MGCA magazine; others resulted from interviews and correspondence with MGCA members specializing in vegetables. Read on...and get growing a Garden of Eatin'!

This book is divided into three sections — first, illustrated hints and tips in A to Z order...then a listing of garden "friends" and "enemies" (see "Companion planting")...and finally a section outlining specific harvesting hints and storage instructions for over 50 vegetables, a fact-filled guide you'll refer to again and again.

7

Wide-row planting of bush beans doubles the normal yield by eliminating rows. See additional photograph and planting instructions under "Bean Hints," page 15, and photograph of peas grown in a similar manner under "Pea Hints," page 58.

A GARDEN WITHOUT ROWS? Intensive gardening utilizes all available garden space. This space-saving method is based on the commercial French Intensive Method developed in the 1890s, and later, after being modified to meet the needs of the home gardener, was first popularized in California. It is now spreading throughout the country. Intensive gardening eliminates rows. Vegetables are closely spaced (many types just a few inches apart) and grown across the entire bed just far enough apart so that outer leaves touch when they reach maturity. *Yields typically are increased 4 to 7 times compared to single row planting in the same space.* In one square foot you can grow as many carrots as you can in a 12-foot row in a conventional garden. First, divide the garden plot into sections and subsections — usually squares or rectangles — that range in size from 3 to 5 feet for root and leaf crops, 3 feet for bush peas and beans and 1-1/2 feet wide for vertical crops like tall peas, pole beans, cucumbers and staked tomatoes. The sections may be mounded and framed with 2 x 4s. Provide pathways for access for special beds more than 5 to 6 feet wide, such as one for corn which can be grown 8" apart. Be sure to add compost or manure, bone meal and wood ashes (or some substitute) so that the soil is superfertile and of good texture. Conventional cultivation and mulching are not required. As plants grow, overlapping leaves shade out and prevent most weed growth. If you'd like more details, you'll find them in *The Postage Stamp Garden Book* by Duane Newcomb (J. P. Tarcher, Inc., 9110 Sunset Blvd., Los Angeles, CA 90069). (See "Stagger rows . . . ")

ALUMINUM FOIL can make your gardening brighter. When spread on soil around plants or on top of mulch, it reflects light and increases photosynthesis of leaves so that crop production is much greater. Tests show that this reflection also repels aphids and flea beetles. They are confused by what appears to them to be a second sky and they take off for your neighbor's garden. Although too expensive to be used extensively, try a test strip or two between rows in a shadier spot in the garden. Or place a square piece of foil around an eggplant or pepper as mulch. Anchor with rocks or with wire coat hangers (snip off top and bend remaining wire into an upside down "U" shape — you can use these again, covered with clear plastic, like hotcaps in early spring.) (See "Plant tents.") Square of foil at base of squash repels squash vine borers.

ALUMINUM FOIL "SUN BOXES." Lack of sun in early spring causing a problem starting vegetables indoors? Some gardeners just flick on their fluorescents (see "Zero weather"). If you don't have indoor lights, you can "make do" by setting your plants in cardboard boxes with the fronts cut out and the backs and sides lined with aluminum foil. When set near windows, the foil reflects light back on the plants; stems grow straight instead of leaning toward the sun. These "sun boxes" also come in handy during the hardening-off process. In windy or cold weather, slip boxes inside plastic dry cleaning bags and you have a miniature, portable greenhouse.

ANALYZED YOUR SOIL HEALTH LATELY? A soil test can spot nitrogen, phosphorus, potassium and other deficiencies, tell you the pH reading (acidity vs. alkalinity) — and thus can help you get started on correcting what may be out of balance. County agricultural extension services often provide professional soil testing services for a small fee. For instant, on-the-spot analysis, invest in the best soil testing kit you can afford. Some gardeners "tailor" the soil to meet the needs of individual crops. Asparagus, beets, broccoli, cauliflower, cabbage and muskmelons grow best in soil above the neutral (7.0) range — up to 8.0 (alkaline); beans, peas, tomatoes, carrots, cucumbers and corn prefer a pH factor of 5.5 - 6.8 (slightly acid); potatoes, eggplant, watermelon, rhubarb, raspberries and endive prefer a more acid soil — in the 5.0 - 6.8 range. Ground dolomitic limestone or agricultural lime will "sweeten" an acid soil; when the soil is too alkaline, apply powdered sulfur — use either carefully; stick to recommended rates. In general, goal should be to maintain the proper *balance* of nutrients in the soil, *as lack of a single nutrient holds back growth even if other nutrients are available in abundant supply*. In addition to the "big three" nutrients mentioned above, a healthy soil also needs calcium, magnesium and sulfur. All can be provided by compost and balanced fertilizers. Micronutrients or trace elements such as iron, manganese and boron usually are available in sufficient amounts but can be assured by addition of animal manure, leaves and other organic matter. (See "Composting," "Fertilizer *faux pas*," "Hunger signs," "Leaves" and "Lime.")

9

ANXIOUS TO GET GOING? Knowing *when* to plant each vegetable is a "must" for a more productive garden. Once you know the average date of the last killing frost in your immediate area, you can determine the sequence of planting. Frost maps in gardening books and seed catalogs may be used only as a general guideline. First-time gardeners should *inquire locally;* frost dates can vary from county to county. Arizona, for example, is divided into five different micro-climates with the date of the last killing frost ranging from February 1-28 to May 15-31. Follow these general tips:

- MOTHER NATURE'S PLANTING GUIDE: (1) plant peas and other cool season crops once color first develops in tulips and other spring bulbs; (2) mid-season crops such as bush beans and early corn can go in when first leaves appear on the trees; (3) hold off planting warm season crops such as tomatoes and squash until blossoms appear on apple, cherry, quince and strawberries.

- PLANTING CLASSIFICATION ACCORDING TO HARDINESS:

  HARDY [plant as soon as ground can be worked in the spring — roughly 20-40 days before the last killing frost; in warm weather areas these crops may be planted from fall to early spring]: broccoli plants* , Brussels sprouts, cabbage plants* , celeriac, celery* , Chinese cabbage* , collards* , garlic, kale* , kohlrabi* , mustard* , onions* , peas* , radishes* , rutabagas* , spinach* , strawberries, turnips* .

  SEMI-HARDY [plant a week or two after those classified as "Hardy" — about 10-30 days before the last killing frost]: beets* , carrots* , cauliflower* , endive* , lettuce* , parsley, parsnips, potatoes, salsify, Swiss chard.

  TENDER [plant on or about the average date of last killing frost]: bush* and pole beans, sweet corn, cucumbers* , horseradish, Jerusalem artichokes, hot weather spinach, summer squash* .

  VERY TENDER [wait until the soil has warmed up — usually about 10-20 days after the average date of the last killing frost]: lima beans, soy beans, crowder/field/southern peas, eggplant, gourds, okra, peanuts, peppers, pumpkin, winter squash* , sweet potatoes, tomatoes, muskmelons [cantaloupe], Crenshaw melons, watermelons.

- PLANT SECOND CROP OF FAST-MATURING VARIETIES FOR FALL HARVEST. Vegetables identified with an asterisk above may, in many areas, be re-planted in late June to August for a late crop. Count back from the average date of the first killing frost in the fall; pick quick-maturing varieties (60-70 days). In planning a fall garden, remember that summer plantings generally mature more rapidly than spring-planted crops. Days to maturity on seed packets refer to *spring-sown seed* (see "Leave enough time" and "Seed starting hints"). Salad Bowl and Oak Leaf lettuce are dependable for long harvests (covered with hay or leaves on cold nights). Zucchini Elite matures in just 48 days.

- IN GENERAL, RISK EXTRA-EARLY PLANTING AND LATER-THAN-USUAL SUMMER SOWING, TOO. Try corn 3-7 days before the average date of spring's last killing frost — plant as deep as 1-1/2" to avoid freezing. Loose hay or straw will provide early protection. It's foolish, however, to plant heat-loving plants such as limas, eggplant, melons and tomatoes *before the soil warms up*. Plants will just sulk; seeds probably will rot.

APHIDS are an A-1 treat for ladybugs. They can eat up to 100 a day and still be hungry for more. If you order ladybugs by mail, you can keep 'em dormant in the refrigerator for three or more months and release only a handful at a time. Occasionally sprinkle ladybug bag with water. Also try rotenone or pyrethrum and see pages 8, 36, 42, 55, 77 and 87.

AQUARIUM WATER is rich in nutrients. Empty it around vegetables or roses; use it when transplanting.

ARRANGE SEED PACKETS into three "when to plant" stacks — early, midseason, late.

ASHES (unleached) are handy in the garden and in the compost heap. Wood ashes contain about 7% potassium and 1.5% phosphorus. Ashes from twigs are richer than those from mature wood. Also useful as insect repellent or otherwise beneficial around zucchini, cabbage, beets and turnips (prevents scab), onions, carrots, beans, peas, lettuce and corn (strengthens stalks). Spread a few inches from plants (avoid ashes around germinating seeds, however); dig into soil.

ASPARAGUS BEETLES bugging you? Try: (1) handpicking early in the morning (dew-covered beetles can't fly); (2) using 1% rotenone dust or Sevin* throughout growing season; (3) planting tomatoes or calendulas nearby; (4) sprinkling salt on soil (this dries up any of the sluglike larvae crawling from spears and also helps to keep down weeds); (5) letting poultry loose in the asparagus patch — they love beetles and larvae; (6) practice garden cleanliness and fall rototilling to prevent beetles from overwintering; (7) dust plantings with bone meal or rock phosphate.

---

* Or Sevin-50W, a 50% wettable powder safe to use one day before harvest. Sevin, although safe for humans, is highly toxic to bees so avoid use around cucumbers, squash and other flowering crops except during the late afternoon after blossoms close. For organic substitute harmless to bees, see page 29.

ASPARAGUS HINTS. Deep 18″ planting no longer is felt to be necessary; 8-10 inches below ground is sufficient. As root stocks grow somewhat closer to the surface as the years go by, this depth provides sufficient protection against injury during cultivation and assures that the plants won't suffer during drought. Asparagus harvest can be spread over a longer period by: (1) uncovering winter mulch from only a third or half of the asparagus bed at one time or (2) by planting crowns at different depths (1-2″ difference) when first set out. Some gardeners use the area intended for a future asparagus bed to grow a root crop that requires frequent cultivation. Perennial weeds will

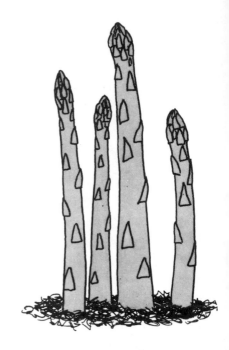

present little or no problem thereafter. If they do, use dacthal (available at garden centers). One-year crowns are generally recommended for better ultimate yields (they'll outproduce two-year crowns in the long run). About 30-50 plants should be sufficient for a family of four. As asparagus is a perennial and a single planting can grow for 15 or more years, pick a well-drained spot off to the side of the garden that will not interfere with rototilling or rotation schedules. A new bed should not have spears cut the first year. The second year, spears as big around as your thumb may be removed over a period of not more than two weeks. In the third year, cutting should last only 4-6 weeks. In subsequent years, harvest can be extended to about 8 weeks. When picking, spears should be snapped off wherever they break off easily (cutting below soil level decreases yield). An asparagus cutter on hand makes a handy tool for digging deep-rooted perennial weeds like dandelion — or for digging carrots. Feed twice annually — in very early spring and after harvest.

A TRIO OF TRICKS TO INCREASE PRODUCTION. Average vegetable garden's yield can be DOUBLED or TRIPLED by trying the following trio of tricks for getting the most out of every inch of growing space (also see "A garden without rows?" and "Vertical gardening"):

- INTERCROPPING OR INTERPLANTING. Plant quick-maturing crops such as leaf lettuce, radishes, spinach, kohlrabi and green

Photograph [opposite page]: Ten different vegetables — cabbage, peas, onions, radishes, carrots, pole beans, tomatoes, cucumbers, cantaloupes, icebox-size watermelons — were grown in an 8-foot diameter "circle of crops." Free reprints of a "how-to-do-it" National Garden Bureau article are available upon request to MGCA National Headquarters [for address, see page 2].

onions between slower-maturing crops. This can be done between *plants* (such as tomatoes, peppers and eggplants) or between *rows* (such as corn). You'll harvest these early crops before the late-maturing vegetables crowd them out. You also can start new seeds or transplants growing alongside established plants. When the original crop is harvested, the new crop fills in the space. Examples: plant lettuce, spinach, radishes and early beans among eggplant, peppers, melons and tomatoes; lettuce or cabbage with bush beans; early corn with tomatoes, okra, bush squash, peanuts or bush sweet potatoes. Plant double pea rows 4-6 feet apart; later, put in two rows of corn between the peas.

- SUCCESSION PLANTING OR DOUBLE CROPPING. Once you've harvested an early crop, fertilize and put in another. Follow lettuce, peas or spinach with beans; harvest broccoli and plant corn (in warmer climates); as you pull cabbage, sow carrot seeds in the same place. In colder climates, harvest early spinach in late spring and then plant beans. When cooler weather arrives, follow beans with another planting of spinach. Lettuce, chard, cabbage, cauliflower and spinach grow well in area previously occupied by nitrogen-producing peas or beans (see "Inoculating legumes"). In fact, almost everything does. Two rules to follow: root crops should succeed top crops and vice versa; cabbage family members shouldn't follow each other. Maintain a "nursery" inside under lights or in a sunny window to keep new, husky transplants coming.

• CATCH CROPPING. Related to both intercropping and succession planting, this practice involves growing fast-maturing crops in spots previously occupied by just-harvested slower-growing vegetables. In colder climates, check the average date for the first killing frost and count backwards based on the maturity time of the replacement crop. Seeds or transplants can be put in before the original crop is ready to be harvested or you can move in "newcomers" regularly — as soon as early crops are harvested. Again, fertilize before replanting. *Keep in mind this rule: don't leave bare ground unplanted; this will just invite weeds.*

BACILLUS THURINGIENSIS (B.T.). Riddled cabbage? Broccoli crawling with green caterpillars? You've got the cabbage worm, one of the hungriest and most damaging garden pests. B.T. was introduced in the early 1960s and can give you, perhaps for the first time, perfect specimens of cabbage and other members of the cabbage family. Now widely used, it is a non-harmful *bacterium* which is a disease for caterpillars only. Eaten by the caterpillar, it forms a toxin in stomach cells; caterpillars are paralyzed and damage to crops stops in about 24 hours. Harmless to man and pets, it may be applied up to day of harvest. Use every 4-5 days (one tablespoon with four gallons of water)

once egg clusters hatch. Apply with a watering can or hose spray attachment. Also controls that ugly, the tomato hornworm — plus gypsy moths, cankerworms, tent caterpillars, cabbage loopers and corn ear worm. Sold at garden centers under various trade names (Dipel, Biotrol, Thuricide, Ferti-lome Worm Spray). (See "Cabbage butterflies.")

BANANA PEELS shouldn't be pitched. Use in compost heap or chop into small pieces and bury around tomatoes, eggplants and peppers — or around roses (no more than three banana peels per bush at one time). Banana peels provide 3.25% phosphorus and 41.76% potash. Result: *higher yields; stronger stems* and *better blooms* on roses.

BASIL planted near tomatoes helps growth and adds flavor to tomatoes — plus repels harmful insects. Ideal herb for drying.

BEAN BEETLES and other pests can be chased off with an Octagon soap spray. Soak the soap overnight in the water to be used for spraying. Spray from the bottom up and wet the leaves thoroughly. Spray from both sides of the row. Apply every 5-7 days; repeat after a rain.

BEAN HINTS. Plant bush and pole varieties concurrently for a continuous harvest. As bush beans play out, pole beans are just coming in. For canning, make later sowings of bush beans. Tenderpod, Tendercrop and Blue Lake are excellent bush varieties. Kentucky Wonder and Blue Lake are recommended pole beans. Try other types, too — Italian Romano, yellow-podded wax beans, broad/fava beans and others. Train pole beans vertically, never horizontally (or they will twist tightly around each other and choke themselves out). Bush beans require little or no fertilization boost; pole beans and lima beans, however, are heavier feeders and welcome a side dressing once  blossoms begin to form. For maximum yields: (1) PICK REGULARLY; (2) INOCULATE THE SEEDS (see "Inoculating Legumes") and (3) CONVERT TO WIDE-ROW PLANTING*, which employs a long band of closely spaced seeds rather than widely spaced rows. WIDTH of row can range from 10" — 4 feet; LENGTH of row is optional. Sow a bean seed every 2-1/2 — 3 inches across width of planting area; move down 6" and plant another wide row. Later thin to 6" between plants.

BEAN SECOND CROP BEFORE FROST? When the leaves of pole beans start to fall off, take off *all* the leaves. Loosen soil around base of plants; boost area with lots of compost. Mix up a few buckets of manure "tea" and let it brew a few days. Pour around plants, let soak in . . . then give a deep watering. New blossoms should show in a few days. Results: about a 60% second crop, a welcome bonus for the freezer. If an early frost nips this plan in the bud, all is not wasted. Dig under nitrogen-rich bean plants or use as mulch around carrots and other late crops.

* Photograph above shows 294 bush bean plants grown in a 2-1/2 x 24' space — twice the number of plants compared to a traditional row planting with 18" spacing between rows [also see photograph on page 8]. Wide-row technique works equally well with peas [see photograph, page 58], carrots, lettuce and other crops. For more information, see "Down-to-Earth Vegetable Gardening Know-How" featuring Dick Raymond [Garden Way Publishing, Charlotte, Vermont 05445].

BEER — see "Slugs a problem?"

BEET AND SWISS CHARD "SEEDS" are actually clusters of seeds — so sow *thinly* (one seed per foot for chard and about six or seven seeds per foot for beets) and thin *early*. Allow only one seedling to grow. Beets don't have the strength to push through crusted soil; cover lightly with peat moss mixed with sand. For extra early beets, start seed indoors. Try Detroit Dark Red, Long Season, Little Egypt and Early Wonder.

BIRD BATH in the vegetable garden attracts insect-eating birds. Place it near cucumbers or melons, which will welcome extra water when bird bath water is replaced daily. Mount a bird feeder at the edge of the garden atop a tall pole and grow gourds or nasturtiums up it (if squirrels start stealing seed, throw in a few moth balls). Place a wren house in amongst the tomatoes for a built-in de-bugger (see photo, page 33).

BLACK PLASTIC MULCH keeps soil warmer, retains moisture and prevents weeds. Plant heat-loving plants like cantaloupes in slits cut in plastic (add sharp sand — the type available from many construction firms — to soil before mulching). Cover plastic with light layer of soil or organic mulch for better appearance (see "Mulching Tips").

BLOSSOM-END ROT ON TOMATOES — generally caused by poor distribution of moisture during particularly hot weather — causes the blossom-end of the tomato to turn grey, then black. Control blossom-end rot with a spray of calcium chloride (1 tablespoon per gallon of water) — and by mulching once blossoming begins.

BROCCOLI HINTS. A cool season crop, broccoli is one of the easiest vegetables to start under lights and does well planted in early spring and again in midsummer for a fall crop. Set out transplants about 18" apart; at the same time, plant two broccoli *seeds* between each plant for a fall crop. Give it some fish emulsion at least once before the heads start to form. Signs of any yellow

blossoms on the head indicate overmaturity. First cutting of broccoli (when florets are in tight bud) should include about 6-8 inches of stem — cut below second pair of leaves below flower head. High cutting retards growth of lateral heads. Problem: green cabbage worms, but these can be virtually eliminated with *Bacillus thuringiensis* described earlier. If you don't use B.T., soaking broccoli in a salt solution (4 teaspoons salt to 1 gallon of cold water) will dislodge most of the critters. Rinse well. Strike stems against side of sink to further dislodge. Soak cauliflower in the same manner. *Cabbage worms are shown below.*

BRUSSELS SPROUTS on the upper part of the plant will grow faster and attain larger size if you pinch out the growing points in the top of each plant about mid-September (in most climates). When small heads first form, start removing leaves from the bottom — 6" up at first, then 3-4" at a time as plant grows. Remove all leaves except those at the top.

BUG TRAPS. Boards, shingles, slices of raw potato and leaves from lettuce, spinach and cabbage placed around the garden at night serve as "traps" for squash bugs, slugs, grubs, cutworms and other nocturnal feeders. They'll crawl under to escape the heat of the day. Collect and destroy in the morning.

BUNDLE OF CORNSTALKS, pipes, tubes of wire mesh — all can serve as "ventilating stacks" to get more air into your compost pile.

BURIED TREASURE Bury kitchen greens and garden trimmings between rows to build up soil fertility. . .or use in compost pile (cover with soil). Keep a half-gallon plastic ice cream container with lid in the kitchen for convenient daily collecting.

C ABBAGE BUTTERFLIES — as they flit from broccoli, to cabbage, to kohlrabi, to cauliflower — leave a trail of egg clusters (destroy these when you spot 'em). Green larvae emerge in just a few days and damage begins. The creamy white cabbage butterflies are fast and elusive, but you can swat them with a tennis racket or catch 'em with a butterfly net. . .or try swinging a 7-foot tomato stake if they keep flitting out of reach. Good exercise! *Also be on the lookout for the medium-size, gray moth shown above [right]. It produces the equally-hungry cabbage looper.*

CABBAGE HINTS. Ideal for starting indoors; start seedlings about 3-4 weeks before projected planting time. Cabbage is hardy and can be set out early. Plant seedlings deeper than previous soil level; solid, low-growing heads will result. Space fall transplants further apart (18-24") than spring transplants  (15-18") — as late cabbage typically is larger. If you prefer smaller heads, plant somewhat closer. Cabbage expert reports that clipping off upper half of leaves with scissors when transplanting avoids wilting, setback. Cabbage loves manure and a high-nitrogen fertilizer such as cottonseed meal or dried blood between rows. Take it easy, however, as *too much* fertilizer can cause heads to crack. Like cauliflower and cucumbers, cabbage needs lots of water. Heads are ready to pick when they are solid and have not begun to split. If cabbage seems to come on all at once, stop further growth by pulling up the plant slightly from the ground until you hear a few roots snapping. This also is recommended in areas with considerable rain. Too much water taken in by roots can cause cabbage to split. Harvest cabbage by carefully cutting the head off at the base, leaving the root and a few large leaves. Small "mini" heads will form and these are tasty. Try interplanting with sage, which gives off camphor that repels cabbage butterflies. Mint also is a repellent — some gardeners place pulled-up mint leaves on top of cabbage heads. Some gardeners have had success repelling cabbage worms by sprinkling a mixture of 1/2-cup of salt with 1 cup of flour on plants early in the morning when dew is on the plants — salt is a repellent, flour dries up the worms. Salt also may be mixed with water and sprayed. . .or just sprinkled with a salt shaker. Another formula that works: Mix 1 quart wood ashes with 1 quart flour and 1 small cup of fine table salt and dust the plants. If you've had a real cabbage worm problem, see "Bacillus thuringiensis."

CANNING TIP FOR TOMATOES (whole, chopped, juice, sauce, paste or pureé processed in a boiling water canner). Add lemon juice or vinegar to each jar — 1 tablespoon per quart, 1 teaspoon per pint. This increases the acid content sufficiently to prevent growth of harmful microorganisms, particularly important with low-acid varieties.

CANOPIES OF NYLON NETTING AND OTHER MATERIALS can control a variety of problems — from hungry birds to cabbage worms. Nylon netting can keep sparrows and other birds, as one California MGCA gardener tells it, "from tossing their own salad with my lettuce plants." He covers all new plantings with the protective netting and raises supports to keep pace with plant growth. Cucumber beetle can be outwitted by tight-fitting cheesecloth, nylon net or plastic netting frame over cucumbers, melons and squash. Raise as plants grow. Try similar canopies over cauliflower, broccoli and cabbage beds to prevent the cabbage butterflies from laying egg clusters. Nylon netting also can be spread over newly-seeded areas as protection against marauding birds and can even be used to protect onions, radishes, turnips, etc. from flies that deposit eggs of root maggots. (See "Wire covers" and "Lizards and snakes.")

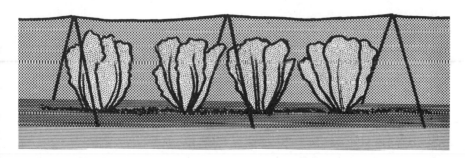

CANTALOUPE* OR PUMPKIN can be planted with the early corn; fruits will have ample sun to ripen once corn is harvested. Space pumpkins 6' apart in rows 7' wide.

CANTALOUPE "SLING." If cantaloupes are trained on trellis (see "Vertical gardening"), a sling to support ripening fruit can be made with margarine tubs and string or from nylon hose (also use for icebox-size watermelons and larger gourds). After growing season, use nylon hose — hung like a Christmas stocking — to store winter onions or gladiolus bulbs.

* "Cantaloupe" is a small, quickly perishable muskmelon [first grown at Cantalupo, an Italian castle]. The true "cantaloupe" is rarely grown in America, but because of its more popular usage "cantaloupe" is used interchangeably in this volume with "muskmelon."

CARROT HINTS. Sow early, after preparing soil to a depth of 10 inches. Remove stones and other debris with a steel rake. Since carrots are slow to germinate, try mixing carrot and Icicle radish seeds together — radishes will mark the row. As you pull radishes, you thin the carrots at the same time and carrots can expand into holes left by radishes. Sand mixed with carrot seed also allows better spacing. Try mixing one cup of *unused* coffee grounds with a package of carrot seeds — mixing helps space tiny carrot seeds to minimize later thinning; coffee aroma in soil repels the root maggot. Sprinkle coffee grounds on the soil during growing season. Carrots should be pulled before they are even half grown: "the biggest isn't the best" applies more to carrots than to any other crop. Try thinning to 2" apart, then later to 4" — meanwhile you can enjoy the delicious "fingerlings" cooked whole. Early carrots may be harvested when the root tops are barely visible above ground. One MGCA carrot expert reports: "If I had to choose but one carrot to grow, it would probably be Scarlet Nantes because it is of top quality and adaptable to most soils." Half Longs also are recommended. Plant succession crops every few weeks until August. As carrots push up out of ground, cover tips with soil. Remove tops when harvesting to prevent wilting. (See "Raised beds" and "Straw-grown carrots.")

CAULIFLOWER HINTS. Plant to mature in early summer or in fall. Unless cauliflower gets plenty of water, heads will be small. It won't tolerate even partially dry soil. Try a 1-2" depression around each plant to catch and hold water...and mulch heavily. Space 18-24" for best growth. Heavy feeder. Purple-headed cauliflower doesn't require "blanching" — shielding the head from the sun to keep it from turning green. To blanch standard varieties, tie outer leaves loosely up over the head with twine or a rubber band when the head is between the size of an egg and a baseball or you can simply bend in a leaf (break slightly) from four sides and tuck them in. Look into the new self-blanching type — its wrapper leaves curl over the heads, protecting them from sunlight automatically. This variety produces over a longer season than many varieties, a real advantage, but heads are somewhat smaller than Snowball or Snow King. When heads are 1-2" in diameter, try enclosing plant with a nylon hose and tie below the head for worm and egg-free harvests. (See "Bacillus thuringiensis," "Cabbage butterflies" and soaking tip under "Broccoli hints.")

CAYENNE PEPPER sprinkled on corn silks and partially-eaten ears as well as foliage of beans, tender tomato plants and other crops repels rabbits, squirrels, raccoons, chipmunks, woodchucks and birds.

CHILD'S SLED - the lightweight, shallow "toboggan" type — makes a roomy, portable "carrier" for a collection of plants started in individual peat pots or expandable peat pellets. If sled is no longer used, punch drainage holes and it's a seedling flat. Another MGCA gardener uses styrofoam containers discarded by typewriter or office supply dealers as a transplanting "flat": "These are deeper than standard flats, are sturdy and light and, if carefully watered, need not even be perforated for drainage. Thus they can be placed where other flats would cause water damage."

CHINESE CABBAGE (Celery Cabbage) — look into this increasingly popular vegetable, which looks like cabbage (with stalks resembling Swiss chard) and tastes like celery. Used in salads, for slaws or cooked like spinach, Chinese cabbage is strictly a cool-season vegetable. For a fall crop sow seed in midsummer in a spot vacated by an early-season crop. If space is a problem, grow it in the flower bed. Needs rich soil, plenty of water. Early varieties mature in 50-60 days, so they're suitable even for northern gardens.

CHINESE CUCUMBERS (also called Oriental or Japanese cucumbers) produce fruit three times the length of traditional varieties — and even if allowed to grow huge don't lose flavor or quality. Burpless, too. Plan on a trellis for these because of their extreme length (up to 20" — although best harvested when about 12" long and about an inch in diameter). When you thin, cut off plants at ground level with a sharp knife or you'll injure root systems of adjoining plants (same advice applies to any cucumber or similar vining crop). Train the vines up the trellis during the hottest part of the day when they're wilted and soft. (See "Cucumber hints.")

CHIVES — take up part of a cluster in the fall and plant it in a pot indoors for continued harvest all winter.

CHRYSANTHEMUMS — plant a few in vegetable garden borders. Mums show wilting from lack of water before any other plants and thus can tell you at a glance when the garden needs water.

CIRCULAR, THREE-TIERED PYRAMID BEDS hold 50 strawberry plants in 6-foot space (equivalent of 28 square feet of growing area). Also handy as decorative accent at corner of garden for salad garden or flowers such as red, white and blue petunias. Available through garden centers and seed supply firms. Accessories include built-in water sprinkler, plastic frost cover and netting to protect strawberries from robin raids. Consider building your own with metal lawn edging or even railroad ties. (See photograph, page 41.)

CIRCUS IN TOWN? Check with a local circus, wildlife park or zoo and you'll find that exotic animal manure is available for the taking. Elephant manure is said to produce mammoth-sized tomatoes.

CLAY FLOWER POTS — try sinking these to the rim alongside squash, cucumber, tomatoes, melons and other plants with a terrible thirst. Water drains slowly through hole at bottom. Or use coffee cans.*

CLOTHESPINS (spring-clip) or paperclips — use to make seed packets spill proof while handling in the garden.

COFFEE GROUNDS — sprinkle on soil around melons, carrots and other crops to repel pests. Nutrient value makes these doubly valuable.

COLD FRAMES AND HOT BEDS are handy to have around to start flower and vegetable seeds, harden off seedlings, as a winter bed for lettuce and for other purposes. Check gardening books in your library for construction details and various ways to use. An inexpensive cold frame can be made to fit a discarded storm sash, as shown in the design by a Staten Island MGCA member reproduced on the opposite page.

COLLECT COFFEE CANS. Use for: (1) starting seeds (punch holes in bottom); (2) storing seed packets (seal with tape and place in 2-pound can with plastic lid); (3) attracting atmospheric magnetic electricity for better growth*; (4) watering gauge (set 1-pound cans under far reaches of sprinkler — one inch accumulation means an inch of water applied to soil); (5) cutting perfect round planting holes in black plastic; (6) root watering devices*; (7) garage storage devices for plant stakes, tools (cut out both ends; nail to garage studs); (8) holding cantaloupes and small watermelons off the ground. Push can into ground about half its height. These add heat and you can get ripe fruit about a week earlier. *Zilched idea* — don't use 2-pound coffee cans in early spring as frost protectors! Afternoon sun reflected off shiny inside surface heats 'em up too fast and damages or kills tender plants, even with plastic lid off.

* **See "Electroculture."**

ONE-SASH COLD FRAME

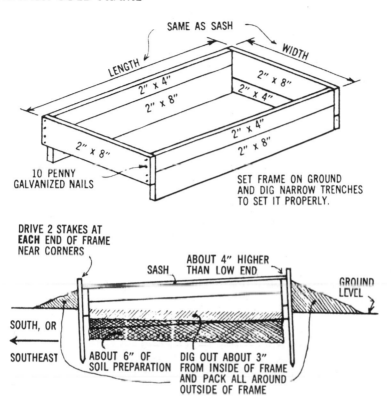

OPERATION

Put sash on frame about February 1st. Sow seeds like marigolds and cabbage about March 15; zinnias and tomatoes about April 1. Plant directly in frame or in flats. Raise sash about 3" at lower end during day to prevent overheating. If weather report says frost, cover sash and frame with an old blanket at night. Transplant seedlings when first pair of true leaves are formed.

During summer, use frame as a small flower bed; **OR** put a shade about 3 ft. over the frame and use for propagating cuttings.

MATERIALS—2 pc. 2" x 4", 8 ft. long
2 pc. 2" x 8", 8 ft. long
1 Sash 3 x 5 ft. (or 2-1/2 x 4-1/2 ft.)
Nails

COMPANION PLANTING or symbiosis — the growing together of "good" neighbors which benefit one another and the separation of "bad" neighbors — is one of the secrets of a more vigorous (and probably happier) garden. All plants give off root diffusates, which affect other plants favorably or unfavorably. The onion family, for example, retards growth of peas and beans but has a beneficial effect on broccoli. Try a "zig zag" planting arrangement to get "friends" closer together. *See SECTION 2 for a roundup of common garden friends and enemies; refer to this list as you plan your garden.*

"COMPOST DIPSTICK" is suggested by *Organic Gardening and Farming.* Use a wooden stake long enough to penetrate to the bottom of the pile. It'll be *hot and damp* if the pile is still "working"; *cool and wet* if it's finished. If dry, you need to reactivate decomposition process.

COMPOSTING — the backyard variety — has many myths and mysteries.

- After trying traditional methods, here's the successful system advocated by a California MGCA member:

  1. Compost bin is made of tight, one-inch redwood boards nailed on three sides to redwood posts. Wood exposed to compost and in the ground is treated* Size: 4' square and about 4' high. Bin is closed by adding boards held in place by cleats inside the two front posts. ("More air is admitted through wire or other enclosures, but excess air also evaporates the moisture and decomposition stops.")

  2. Pile is built up in 6-8" layers as material is available. For added aeration, a long-handled spading fork is used to "fluff-up" and turn the material before each new layer is added ("at least two turnings between layers, 3-4 days apart").

  3. All material is shredded for faster decomposition. (If you don't have a shredder, try spreading leaves out on the driveway and shred with lawn mower; set up a large cardboard box to catch leaves.) A mixture of dry and green materials is ideal. Fresh grass clippings, unless mixed with other materials, will ferment and form a sticky mass.

  4. As activators, a generous handful of nitrogen fertilizer and two or three shovelfuls of manure are applied to each layer.

* **Copper napthanate**

(Topping each layer with soil is not recommended — "the weight of that much soil compacts the mass and drives out the air.") Dried cow or sheep manure may be substituted for fresh if it is not available from local stables.

5. Moisture is added *before* material is added to the pile. Material is saturated, shaken up with the spading fork and left to drain for about an hour. Damp material is "fluffed up" again as it is added to the pile. Top of pile is then smoothed off with a slope to the front (no basin to catch rain, which can create a heavy, soggy mass) and completely covered with roofing paper or plastic to hold moisture, retain heat and shed rain.

6. Except in low winter temperatures, decomposition begins almost immediately and, in about 24 hours, the compost heap starts to heat.

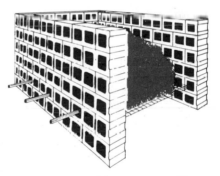

• ALTERNATE CONSTRUC-TION FOR ABOVE-GROUND COMPOST: Use cement blocks with openings facing inside for improved aeration, thrust three iron pipes across the bin, from side to side, through the holes of the second level of blocks from the bottom. This leaves a full 10" space under the pile and this added air circulation *eliminates the need for turning*. Place 1"x2" wire mesh on pipes. Start pile with layer of woody, twiggy cuttings to keep composting materials from seeping down. Shred all materials. Add nitrogen, manure. As the pile heats, cooler air is pulled up from the ground. This air percolates through the mass, aerating it as it passes upward. Compost has been made in ONE WEEK with this raised composting system.

• Don't stop with *one* compost pile. Maintain two or three so you always have compost "working" in various stages. If you shred all materials, keep the heaps moist and add sufficient nitrogen to stimulate and maintain bacterial action (animal manures, dried blood, cottonseed meal, kitchen trimmings, etc.) — you can make compost in 10-14 days. With three compost heaps going, one can be giving you matured compost, the second can be in the process of heating up and the third can be in the "building" stage. A pile thus comes into production every two weeks.

COMPOST made of the tomato's own residues is very beneficial for this plant, a definite peculiarity. Tomatoes don't mind growing in the same place several years as long as the area is kept fertilized.

COMPOST PILE makes an ideal growing medium for cucumbers. Plant them at edge or to grow up sides (if wire enclosure used).

CONSISTENT-SIZE HOLES FOR TRANSPLANTS can be made quickly by using a discarded plastic ice cream scoop instead of a trowel.

CONTINUOUS YEAR-ROUND MULCHING (6-8 inches thick) now has many advocates. No plowing, hoeing, weeding, cultivation. Planting is done by spreading the mulch apart and pushing the seed into the soft soil. Once the plant begins to grow, the mulch is pulled up against it. The heavy layer of decomposing mulch (hay or "anything that rots") provides nutrients like a garden-wide compost pile which, in effect, is what it is. All that's left to do after planting is thinning and picking. Most widely-known practitioner of the system is Ruth Stout, who describes the A to Zs of the system in "How To Have A Green Thumb Without An Aching Back" and in "The Ruth Stout No-Work Garden Book" (Rodale Press, Inc., Emmaus, Pa. 18049).

CORN HINTS. Do try some sweet corn, even if space is limited. Check local sources for tips on which varieties are best for your area. Plant in blocks of at least 3-4 rows (not long single rows) for adequate wind pollination. Corn likes heat, plenty of fertilizer and lots of water. If space is limited, try one or more 4' x 4' "corn beds," with seed planted an inch deep and 8-12" apart. Sweet corn shouldn't be planted next to popcorn or ornamental corn if both have the same maturity date. Separate "super sweet" types such as Illini X-tra Sweet as far as you can from other varieties or you'll lose the extra sweet taste of these varieties.

Removing suckers from corn isn't recommended. You get more ears if you leave the suckers on (and the tassels, too).

- THE EARLIEST SWEET CORN can be planted as soon as the "leaves on the trees are the size of a squirrel's ear," and even earlier (corn sown five weeks ahead of the normal planting time has been successful in Connecticut). Extra-early corn should be sown 1-1/2" deep and not given fertilizer until it's well up. Germination will take place much slower than average because of cool weather — so be patient (you may *still* be the first on your block)! Try warming up the soil early by applying a green plastic mulch a week before planting. Some gardeners lay strips of aluminum foil between the rows to bounce added light on the young plants. Others start seed indoors in individual peat pots.

- MAKE SUCCESSIVE PLANTINGS of one or two preferred varieties rather than plant a number of varieties with different maturities that are not of equal quality. Try this idea from a Minneapolis MGCA member for sweet corn each night at the peak of perfection: Pick an early variety (65 days) and a main crop variety (80 days) . . . and mark your calendar for 12 successive plantings. The first three are of *both* early and main crop varieties, followed by six plantings of the main crop variety. As soon as the soil can be worked, the first planting goes in. The next planting is about a month later for a five-day differential at maturity. Interval between planting is then shortened to five days for the last planting. Result: a continuous supply, with plantings maturing at five-day intervals for two months — until about the first frost.

- FERTILIZING: Corn should be fed with a balanced fertilizer such as 10-6-4, 20-10-10, cottonseed meal or fish emulsion when about 8-10" high — then "hilled" with soil to give support to the roots. Feed again when ears begin to silk.

- CULTIVATION AND HARVEST: Practice light cultivation, as roots are shallow. When ears are harvested, pull up stalk and shred (or stalks will continue to encourage pests and disease — plus take nutrients from the soil and adjoining plants).

- SPURT TEST to determine if sweet corn is ready: Slit the husk slightly while it's still on the stalk, then just prick an exposed kernel with your fingernail. If it acts like a grapefruit, it's ready. Ideally, have water boiling when you go out to pick.

- CORN EAR WORM AND BLACK BEETLES can be prevented by applying several drops of mineral oil to silks at tip of ear as soon as silks begin to dry and turn brown (not before or pollination will be insufficient and you will get undeveloped kernels). Apply about three times at 5-6 day intervals, using a medicine dropper, a pump type oil can with a long spout or a plastic dishwashing detergent bottle. Added benefits: When you husk the ear, most of the silk comes off with the husk;  some say the mineral oil improves the flavor of the corn. Also consider rotenone, Sevin or B.T. (see page 14) as controls. Varieties with long, tight husks minimize the problem.

- CORN SMUT BOILS should be promptly picked and burned. If a neighbor gardens, get him to do the same. Preventive measures: (1) three-year crop rotation; (2) use of disease-resistant varieties such as Silver Queen and Country Gentleman; (3) turning under of garden debris/manure; removal of all corn stalks in the fall.

- WATERING: Determine need for water by appearance and performance of plants, not by the apparent dryness of the soil. Keep in mind this old farming maxim: "Toward maturity, just sufficient water to maintain healthy stalks."

- VARIETIES: Look to local sources for best corn varieties in your area. As with other vegetables, even 100 miles can make a difference. Check into insect and disease resistance, too. If you pick varieties with different maturity dates, be sure each variety is planted close together in a BLOCK (not one long row of one variety, then another row of a second variety).

- ANIMAL PESTS — See "Cayenne pepper," "Raccoons" and "Woodchucks."

CROSSING — See "Varieties."

CUCUMBER HINTS. Don't despair if the first blossoms don't set fruit; cucumbers develop only from female flowers and the first 10-20 plus flowers are male. Look into gynoecious (all-female) varieties.

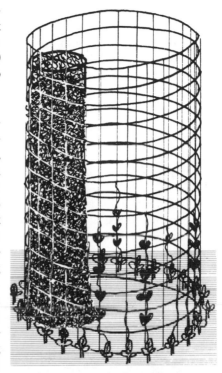

- Cucumbers are space grabbers, so try growing cucumber vines up chicken wire, posts or trellises. Best bet: a "cucumber tree"* — plant seeds an inch deep every 6-8 inches around a 3-4 foot diameter ring of 5-foot high concrete reinforcing wire with 6" mesh (plenty big enough to pick through — don't substitute small mesh wire or many cucumbers will be "trapped" inside). Because cucumbers are among the heaviest feeders, you'll increase production if you give the "cucumber tree" its own compost "pile," i.e. a 4-5 foot ring of chicken wire or welded wire about 1 foot in diameter mounted in the center or tied inside to one side. Fill with grass clippings, manure, etc.; as "compost cone" decomposes, it feeds the close-planted cucumbers.

- Give cucumbers plenty of water during the growing season (they're 96% water); keep mulched to retain moisture. Sink large coffee or shortening can, with nail holes punched in bottom, at time of planting for easy watering (see "Manure tea").

- Pick regularly to keep plants producing. If you overlook a "giant" that's too big for salads or pickling — peel it, slice into 1/2-inch slices, dip into eggplant-type batter and fry. Delicious!

- Spotted and striped cucumber beetles can cause bacterial wilt overnight and completely destroy the crop. Try covering young cucumber plants with hotcaps or cheesecloth netting and plant radishes, onions and French marigolds around plants. Sevin** is also recommended, but be sure to start application as soon as plants emerge. Shallow tins of water and cooking oil will trap 'em.

* See photograph of "cucumber tree" on page 7.

** Organic substitute: one handful each of wood ashes and hydrated lime mixed with two gallons of water; spray all surfaces of leaves. TRY THIS DURING PERIODS WHEN BEES ARE BUSY.

CUTWORMS — foil them with a 3" cardboard collar around stem of tomato, pepper and other susceptible plants. "Collar" should be extended 1" below ground. Cut "collars" from milk cartons or use empty bathroom tissue rolls or frozen juice cans. Or simply stick wooden matchsticks or waxed straws on two sides of the stem. For a built-in cutworm "collar," grow plants in paper cups; punch out bottom and plant. Newspaper strips also may be used (see "Yesterday's newspaper").

AMPING-OFF" A PROBLEM? The wilting and sudden death of seedlings can be avoided in many cases if you:

1. SOW SEEDS IN A STERILE MEDIUM. Vermiculite or sphagnum peat moss alone can be used, but these provide no nutrients — provide supplementary feeding and transplant when first pair of true leaves appear. To save time, try a 50/50 mix of Terra-Lite's "Tomato Soil"* and organic peat. "Tomato Soil," introduced in 1974, is sterile, includes nutrients for vigorous growth and can be used with any plants. Even when thoroughly soaked, this mix permits ample air circulation around plant roots, helping to avoid damping-off problems. Never use garden soil or compost unless it is sterilized first (see "X-tra potent soil for transplants").

2. DUST SEEDS WITH A POWDERED FUNGICIDE such as Benomyl or Captan (mix as much as you can get on the end of a flat toothpick to package of seed).

3. WATER SPARINGLY BETWEEN PLANTS. Avoid getting water directly on the seedlings. Keep soil moist, but not sodden and never allow to dry out. Always use *warm water.*

4. AVOID OVERCROWDING BY SOWING THINLY.

5. PROVIDE GOOD AIR CIRCULATION. Give seedlings fresh air without drafts. Try a small oscillating fan.

6. GROW SEEDLINGS IN A SUNNY WINDOW AT NORMAL ROOM TEMPERATURES. Both low light and too much warmth can cause legginess.

7. IF COOL GRO-LUX-TYPE LIGHTS ARE USED, KEEP LIGHT SOURCE 3-7 INCHES FROM SEEDLINGS. Plants will "stretch" for light too far away — spindly, succulent growth makes seedlings susceptible to fungus.

* **This product, like Burpee's "Tomato Growing Formula" introduced in 1976, is especially recommended for tomatoes, peppers and eggplants.**

8. DISINFECT PLASTIC TRAYS — soak in several gallons of hot soapy water with a cup of Clorox added. Note: To stop "damping-off" process *once it has begun,* heat some fine sand in the oven, sprinkle lightly on soil among uninfected seedlings.

DANDELIONS that come up in the vegetable garden are more tasty in salads than the lawn lovers.

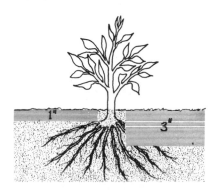

DEEP CULTIVATION destroys roots *and* brings more weeds to the surface where they germinate. Practice shallow cultivation — one inch or less — or eliminate the need for hoeing altogether with mulches.

DIRECTION OF ROWS. Many gardeners run rows north and south to avoid shading, but it really makes little difference which way they run. If rows run east and west, grow corn, staked tomatoes and trellised crops on the north or northeast side. Running rows *lengthwise* of the garden, however, makes cultivation easier. (See "Sloping plot?")

DISEASE-RESISTANT VEGETABLE VARIETIES — look for these in the seed racks or in the catalogs. Also search out varieties marked "AAS" — winners of the All-American Selections Award. These are extra reliable, with excellent quality and taste. Look for "Hybrid" designations, too.

"DO IT TODAY" CARD. Something that needs attention catches your eye as you walk out to the garden. You stop and do whatever it is. When you finish, you notice the tomatoes need staking. . .and so it goes. Result: you don't get the cultivating done, which was Number 1 priority. To avoid distractions, and to assure that the most important job gets done first, maintain a "Do it today" card — a written list of jobs *in priority order* on a 3" x 5" index card. As you notice new things to do, add them to the bottom of the list.

DRAINAGE TEST. Dig a few holes 2-3 feet deep and at different locations in the garden; fill with water. If it drains away immediately, it's too sandy and organic material should be added. If water drains within a period of 1/2 hour to 1 hour, drainage is no problem. If the water still remains after 24 hours, you'll have serious difficulty growing vegetables and should take steps to improve drainage. Add sand, peat moss, compost or other soil conditioning materials.

EARTHWORMS love coffee grounds. Dig grounds into vegetable garden or rose bed. Grounds provide nutrients and also repel pests (see "Coffee grounds").

EDGING (METAL) sunk 6-8" around garden borders keeps grass out.

EDIBLE-PODDED PEAS (also called "sugar peas" and "snow peas") — grow these once and you'll probably be an instant convert. Recommended varieties: Mammoth Melting Sugar (pole), Oregon Sugar Pod (bush) and Dwarf Gray Sugar (bush, earliest, smallest pods).

EGG CARTONS of styrofoam are dandy for starting seeds. Cardboard types, however, absorb too much water and plants dry out too quickly.

EGGPLANT HINTS. For larger eggplants, snip off all but four or five blossoms per plant. If leaves yellow, the plant needs water. Feed lightly every four weeks (overfeeding delays fruit set). Harvest when fruit has a glossy coating. Cut, *do not pull,* the fruit from the plant. Don't grow eggplant where tomatoes, potatoes or eggplant have been grown in the last three years (see "Rotate crops").

EGGSHELLS added to the compost pile will add lime to the soil over a period of years...plus nitrogen and phosphorus.

EGYPTIAN ONIONS, an easy-to-grow perennial, are one of the most intriguing vegetables around. They're called "top-multipliers" because small, edible onions are produced on top of fat, hollow stalks rising three feet. Flavor is distinctive — stronger than chives, but much milder than garlic. Delicious in salads or in cooking. Hollow stems can be chopped for salads or split and stuffed with cream cheese. Bases of the stems are cooked like leeks. When the stalk bends over, the mini bulbs take root and provide scallions in early spring. May be planted in late summer, fall or spring.

Photographs [opposite page]: In Bob Sanders' Des Moines garden, this Yolo Wonder pepper plant surrounded by a metal peony ring and with a metal fence nearby produced 52 bell peppers by the end of the season (control plants without peony rings produced 14-20). In the bottom photograph, metal corn-crib ventilators support smaller volunteer tomato plants; concrete reinforcing wire cylinders surround 7-foot high Better Boy VFN and Golden Boy tomato plants, which produced an average of 150-200 tomatoes per plant. End-of-season, pre-frost harvest from just eight plants completely covered a Ping-pong table (see photo, page 116).

ELECTROCULTURE can put a new spark in your garden. Try some experiments with this successfully-tested practice involving exposure of plants to atmospheric magnetic electricity for "supercharged" growth. Jerry Baker, author of *Plants Are Like People,* explains it succinctly this way: "electrically charged oxygen is turned into 78% nitrogen." Extensive experiments with various vegetables showed increases in yield of from 30 to 70%. Electroculture can be practiced in the home garden by: (1) using metal fencing whenever possible; (2) sinking tin cans with holes punched in bottom and sides 6-8  inches from plant stems (cans may be filled with compost or manure and used for deep watering tomatoes, eggplants, cucumbers, melons, etc.); (3) stretching fine copper wire over a row of vegetables between wooden posts; (4) putting peony rings around broccoli and pepper plants; (5) growing indeterminate tomatoes in concrete reinforcing wire cylinders (see "X-traordinary tomato production" for a description of the method that can produce up to 200 tomatoes per plant).

EPSOM SALTS (MAGNESIUM SULPHATE HEPTAHYDRATE) can help correct a magnesium deficiency in the soil (which is one of several reasons that can cause tomato blossoms to drop). Buy the course type found at drug stores. Use about a handful around plants, scratch into surface. Water after application. Some gardeners use Epsom salts in planting holes for tomatoes, peppers and eggplants; others mix a teaspoon with about a pint or so of lukewarm water and spray it on foliage of pepper and other plants.

EXPERIMENT WITH A NEW VARIETY or a vegetable new to you each growing season. It's fun and you may discover a real favorite. Have you tried edible-podded peas, Swiss chard, salsify, yard-long beans, white eggplant, lemon cucumbers, spaghetti squash, kohlrabi, purple cauliflower, celeriac, kale?

 ALL PRUNINGS can double as pea trellises in the spring. Or use snow fencing (which, incidentally, makes an efficient, portable compost enclosure).

FALL ROTOTILLING puts you a giant step ahead in the spring. Dig under undiseased plant debris, leaves, manure, cut weeds — all the organic material you can find (be a "night stalker" for bountiful bags of leaves left curbside for pickup). Leave ground rough. Finally, put your garden "to bed" as nature does — lay down a mulch of leaves or other organic matter over the entire garden beginning as fast as garden rows are emptied and rototilled. If you use whole leaves, topping with a light scattering of straw or hay will prevent blowing. It's best, however, to shred leaves (run over them with your lawn mower if you don't have a shredder) — they won't scatter and will decompose faster. In the spring, at least 10 days before planting, rake off mulch where you'll be planting early crops to allow ground to warm up and dry out. For faster warm-up, lay down some green plastic on these areas.

FERTILIZER *FAUX PAS:* using lawn fertilizer that's handy in the garage on the vegetable garden. If you use inorganic fertilizers, buy a balanced fertilizer *especially formulated for vegetables* such as Scotts 18-24-6 or Ferti-lome's 6-11-7. Hoffman offers an all-organic vegetable fertilizer (4-4-3). Follow directions on any fertilizer carefully. Organic fertilizers have lower nitrogen, phosphorus and potash ratios, are slower acting and are more welcome by earthworms. Water-soluble, odorless fish emulsion (5-2-2) works wonders with many crops. Cottonseed meal (6-2-2) is an excellent, all-around organic fertilizer (available at feed stores for about $9 per 100#). Dried blood (15-3-0) and blood meal (15-1.3-.7) are useful around nitrogen-loving crops such as lettuce, spinach and cabbage. Rock phosphate adds phosphorus. Apply nitrogen fertilizer only in the spring; otherwise it will be wasted. In general, apply garden fertilizers in frequent, small applications rather than large amounts at long intervals. It's not true that if one application can do "so much" good, that twice as much will be twice as good — just the opposite! *RECOMMENDATION: use the quicker-acting inorganic fertilizers if it's a "first year" garden, with liberal applications of dried sheep manure. Thereafter, build up soil with compost, manure and organic fertilizers and use inorganic fertilizers only as plants seem to need a boost.* (See "Analyzed your soil health lately?" "Composting," "Hunger signs in the garden?" "Leaves," "Lime," and "Manure tea.")

FERTILIZER FORMULA: 100 pounds per acre (a frequently recommended rate) = 1/2 cup per 100 square feet. Figure other proportions from this formula.

"FINGERLING" POTATO is rated by many as the finest for potato salad and German-fried potatoes. Plants produce large quantities of 2-4" long potatoes, only 1" or so in diameter. Yellow skin and flesh. One source: Olds Seed Company (Madison, WI 53701).

FLOPPY FENCES CAN BE AVOIDED by buying sturdy, 4' *welded* wire with 1" X 2" mesh and cutting it lengthwise with wire cutter into 2' high fencing. Cost: $1.44 per foot for 4' ($.72 for 2' height) compared to about $.25 a foot for regular rabbit fencing. Welded wire, however, reduces support stake needs by 66% and — as a bonus — is more long-lasting and attractive. Two-foot height makes an ideal trellis for growing many varieties of peas; plant row on each side. Leftover 4' pieces, mounted vertically, can be used to grow pole beans, cucumbers, etc. — or you can use them to form a sturdy, circular compost enclosure.

FLOWERS AND HERBS IN THE VEGETABLE GARDEN attract bees, therefore helping vegetable pollination. Some flowers, and many herbs, also repel insect pests: French marigolds (cucumber beetles, Mexican bean beetles, nematodes and many other insects), asters, chrysanthemums, cosmos, coreopsis, calendula (around asparagus) and petunia (protects beans). Pyrethrum ("painted daisy," "painted lady") flower heads, dried and powdered, are available commercially in pure form from pet shops and veterinarians as pyrethrum insecticide. Considered the least toxic to man and animals of all insecticides, it quickly paralyzes leafhoppers and a number of other soft-bodied, leaf-eating insects when applied directly on them. When purchased in commercial sprays and dusts, pyrethrum is often mixed with rotenone, an insecticide derived from tropical plants. Also see "Nasturtiums" and "White geraniums."

FREEZING FOR FLAVOR. When you cook peas, broccoli and other summer vegetables for the freezer, *don't throw away the cooking water* (which contains vitamins and the vegetable's sweet flavor). Pour the vegetable *and* its juice into leak-proof container, leaving 1/2" at the top for expansion. Cool container and contents to room temperature before freezing. Because the liquid takes longer to thaw, remove from freezer in the morning. That evening, finish cooking over medium low heat. See "Peas in a pillowcase."

FREEZING TIPS FOR CORN-ON-THE-COB. More and more gardeners are experimenting with freezing corn without blanching first for a "just picked" flavor during the winter (and no sogginess). Simply husk the corn, wrap individually in waxed or freezer paper and enclose in a plastic sack. Others say "why waste the paper?" They remove silks to keep the freezer clean and freeze the corn in its own husk wrapper.

FROST DAMAGE IN AUTUMN can be minimized by covering susceptible plants with a loose mulch such as straw or hay or leaves, or with upside down baskets, burlap bags, clear or black plastic or with old sheets (whatever covers plants — such as sheets — should not touch foliage). The easiest way to get frost protection is *simply by sprinkling.* Spray frost-sensitive tomatoes, peppers and eggplants with a hose on the eve of a frost. Cornell University recommends applying 1/10" of water per hour, beginning when temperature falls near 32° — and wetting foliage at least once a minute until no ice remains. How does it work? Mist crystallizes on the foliage and keeps internal fluids from freezing. If you miss the "night before" treatment, spray the next morning *before the sun strikes the foliage.*

FUNGUS DISEASES — real crop destroyers — can be minimized by:

- Good air circulation (grow pole beans on open trellis rather than tight tripod of bamboo canes if air circulation isn't the best).

- Being as generous as you can with space between plants and between rows.

- Giving plants as much *sunlight* as possible.

- Watering during the morning — and only on sunny days so garden can dry off quickly. Keep garden well drained.

- Handling plants as little as possible — and *never* when they are wet from dew or rain.

- Getting rid of disease-carrying insects and diseased plants promptly (don't leave to wither in place) and *rotating* the next year (see "Rotate crops").

- Mulching to prevent mud splashing up on lower foliage — and thus spreading soil-borne diseases.

- Treating seed with a fungicide... or buying pre-treated seed.

- Taking EARLY ACTION; check with your local MGCA chapter or garden center for advice.

- Looking for disease resistance in seeds and purchased plants (see "Disease-resistant vegetable varieties").

- Remembering that HEALTHY, WELL-FERTILIZED PLANTS ARE LESS LIKELY TO CONTACT FUNGUS DISEASES.

GARDEN NOTEBOOKS AND CALENDARS come in handy. Jot down planting and harvesting dates for reference next year. Use to schedule late summer and fall planting dates in advance — count number of days before expected first killing frost. In a notebook, jot down what did or did not do well, what you want to change, garden areas that need work, reminders about rotating (always keep your garden plan for reference).

GARDEN SCOOPS (for fertilizer, sand, etc.) can be made easily by diagonally cutting off the bottom of various size plastic jugs with handles. After tracing "cut line" with pencil, cut with heavy scissors or tin snips. Leave jug cap on for use as a *scoop;* remove cap and it's a *funnel.*

GARLIC - plant around lettuce and other parts of the vegetable garden to repel aphids and many other pests (excellent around rose bushes). Try a *fall* planting of garlic, too. In Massachusetts, garlic sets planted in early September grew to twice the size of bulbs planted the following spring. Separate into sections and plant 1-1/2" deep and 4" apart in rows 12-14" apart — or just plant randomly. Winter mulch isn't necessary, except in extremely cold sections. Look into *elephant garlic,* too!

GOURDS — grow 'em for fun and fall decoration, for the kids or as trellis ornamentation. Harvest when fully mature; store in a warm, dry place all winter, taking care that the surfaces aren't scratched. Many gardeners pitch out perfectly good gourds *in the mistaken belief they have spoiled.* A dark or light-colored mold *will* appear; this is natural. After thoroughly dry, scrub off mold and any  film (on smooth-surfaced gourds). Paint with shellac and a good paint. The distinctive "caricature" gourds shown here are just part of a MGCA member's collection.

GRASS CLIPPINGS — don't pile clippings too deeply when using as mulch or they'll mat, become slimy and smell. Keep away from stems if wet, as they can heat up and damage or kill plants. Dry out on driveway before applying to garden; spread in thin layers. For best results, mix with straw, hay or leaves in the garden and in the compost heap. Word of warning: avoid clippings from lawn recently treated with 2-4,D.

GRASSHOPPERS — see "Quart jars."

GREEN THUMB — You can bet that if you have a green thumb you have a *busy* thumb as well as *callused palms.*

GROUND CORNCOBS, light and bulky, are useful as a mulch for asparagus and other vegetables. Stockpile them during the sweet corn season; shred once they're dry. Set out the fresh cobs in a bird feeder; blue jays will clean them nicely for you.

GROW GOLD. If you're not doing so, try golden zucchini, Nemagold sweet potatoes, golden beets, golden wax beans (pole or bush), golden eggplant or one of the many golden tomato varieties such as Golden Boy (great canned and makes delicious juice) or Yellow Pear (see photo, page 84), a "mini" pear-shaped tomato ideal for preserves. Look into yellow-fleshed Yellow Baby Watermelon. A dependable producer in short seasons, this unusual hybrid was a 1975 All-America winner.

Yellow Baby Watermelon

H ARDEN OFF TRANSPLANTS grown from seed for about two weeks before setting out in the garden. Set seed flats and potted plants outdoors for short periods (start with an hour or so) — at first in the shade and in a sheltered location. Gradually increase degree of sunlight and length of exposure. Stop watering several days before hardening off; don't overwater once outside. (See "Cold frames and hot beds.")

HARVESTING HINTS. See Section 3 beginning on page 92.

HORSERADISH — plant at corners of potato patch. Repels potato beetles. As horseradish tends to spread, plant in sunken pots.

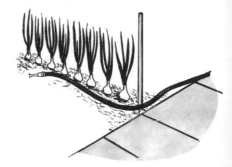

HOSE STAKE — drive sturdy stakes at the ends of rows or other strategic places to eliminate the hose hassle. Dragging a heavy hose through the garden can quickly damage dozens of plants.

HUMAN HAIR provides an excellent nitrogen source for compost heap; many barbers have it by the boxful for the asking. Six or seven pounds of hair contain a pound of nitrogen — or as much as up to 200 pounds of manure.

HUNGER SIGNS IN THE GARDEN? Watch for these... and give the appropriate fertilizer boost. Here are the key "hunger signs" as they show up on certain crops. *Nitrogen deficiency:* slow growth, slender stems, fading yellow foliage. Check the top of tomato plants; they'll start to fade at the tips of the leaves. *Phosphorus deficiency:* slow growth, undersides of leaves are reddish-purple; plants are slow to set fruit and mature. These signs appear on tomatoes. If corn kernels don't fill out to the end of the ear, this typically is another sign of phosphorus shortage. *Potassium deficiency:* Older leaves begin to turn yellow at the edges. Stunted growth and weak stalks are other signs. *Magnesium deficiency:* late maturity; leaf veins remain green, but leaves turn yellow... then brown. Tomatoes have brittle leaves which curl up, then turn yellow. Lima beans, cucumbers, carrots and squash show mottling, then browning of foliage. Corn develops white streaks or yellow striping on only the older leaves. (See "Epsom salts.") *Boron deficiency:* this causes specific changes in different vegetables. Tomato stems, for example, develop blackened areas at the growing point; terminal shoots curl, turn yellow and die. Boron deficiency generally causes bitterness. In general, "hunger signs" will begin to appear after three or four years of consecutive cultivation. Necessary nutrients generally will be available in "first time" gardens.

 CE CUBES — easy way to water outdoor hanging plants of Tiny Tim or Pixie tomatoes. Also try spreading ice cubes on rows of late-planted peas to speed germination.

INOCULATING LEGUMES with nitrogen-fixing bacteria before planting assures more even germination, faster growth, bigger yields. As treatment allows plants to use nitrogen from air, peas and beans become soil *builders*, not *robbers*. Legume interplanting, the growing together of legume and non-legume plants, forces the legume to pick up more nitrogen from the air and, in early tests, has led to better production. Inoculate is very inexpensive and is sold at garden centers and through seed catalogs as "Nitragin" and under other trade names. To inoculate, soak pea and bean seeds in water (see "Seed starting hints"); drain; stir in honey to make inoculate stick better (optional) and sprinkle with culture, a black powder. You'll call it black magic!

INSECT DAMAGE early in the season can sometimes *increase yields,* according to Canadian studies reported in the scientific journal, *Agro-Ecosystems*. Early damage serves to prune some plants effectively and they send out more and healthier shoots.

INTERPLANT FLOWERS AND VEGETABLES. Eggplant, peppers, cherry tomatoes and Rhubarb Swiss chard seem "right at home" in the flower border. Carrot and asparagus "fronds" are attractive among perennials. Strawberries make a good edging. Use parsley, chives, ornamental kale, flowering cabbage or lettuce as edible borders. Try some of these in the rose bed (but *not* if you use sprays or systematics for insect control). (See "Flowers and herbs in the vegetable garden" and "Peanuts.")

41

JAPANESE BEETLES can be controlled biologically by introducing *Bacillus popillae* or "milky spore disease." Perfectly safe, a teaspoon every three feet in the lawn or garden does the job and it lasts for years. It's fatal to the Japanese beetle larvae and generations to come — but is harmless to earthworms. Check your garden center for "Doom."

JETS OF WATER from your garden hose will dislodge and discourage aphids and other bugs. Best to do this in the morning. Hit undersides of leaves, too. Blast 'em twice a day with a hard spray.

KALE is about the heartiest green you can grow. Try a late planting and you won't have as many bug problems. Let it grow on into the winter; brush off snow to harvest. Good in soups, cooked like spinach and chard or raw in salads.

KEROSENE — If hand-picking larger "creepy critters" bothers you, keep a small supply of kerosene handy (but not to children). Beetles and other larger bugs are sluggish in early morning. Using a strip of lath or similar "paddle," simply brush 'em into a can partially filled with the lethal liquid. Or just add a little kerosene to water. Dish detergent and water also may be used.

KOHLRABI, a cousin to the cabbage family, looks like Russia's "Sputnik" satellite when it's growing and maybe that's why shredded kohlrabi is better in borsch than shredded cabbage. Also excellent raw (chill and slice very thinly), marinated in French dressing, pickled, boiled and fried. Kohlrabi likes calcium, so apply a little dolomitic lime or calcific limestone before planting. Don't plant too much kohlrabi at one time as it comes on "all at once" and must be used when young and tender (swollen stem, if larger than 2-2 1/2" in diameter, becomes hard and bitter). Since it's harvested early, try interplanting in early spring between slower growing crops. Does not do well in the heat of summer. Plant more in late summer to mature in cool weather.

LAUNDER YOUR LETTUCE! "I have an old laundry tub set on a concrete block under a higher-than-usual hose bib in the garden, with a simple 'drain board' on one side for washing or scrubbing fresh vegetables before taking into the kitchen."

LEAF-CURL ON TOMATOES is no cause for alarm. It's common on pruned and staked tomatoes and often occurs on hot days and following heavy rains. When plants grow in a "shoestring" fashion, however, it's a mosaic disease (Shoestring Disease) for which there is no control (pull up and burn plants).

LEAVE ENOUGH TIME! "Days to maturity" on seed packets for vegetables suitable for transplanting means *the time to maturity from the setting out of a husky transplant started earlier inside — NOT from the time seed is sown outside.* So count backwards from the projected planting time outside to know *when* to sow seeds indoors. General guide: 8-10 weeks before transplanting (onions, parsley); 7-12 weeks (celeriac, celery); 6-8 weeks (eggplant, peppers, tomatoes); 5-7 weeks (watermelon*, broccoli, Brussels sprouts, cabbage, cauliflower, collards, lettuce); 3-4 weeks (muskmelons*, cucumbers*, summer and winter squash*, sweet potato — from tuber). *Grow these in individual containers such as peat pots (see "Peat Pots") for transplanting without root disturbance. Start with three seeds, later pinch off all but one plant.

LEAVES, pound for pound, have twice as many nutrients (phosphorus, calcium, magnesium and trace minerals) as manure. Shred some extra during the fall abundance and sack for early summer mulch. Leaves (and corn stalks) should be shredded or mixed with loose straw or hay to prevent compacting into a soggy mass. Leaves not needed for mulch may be mixed with grass clippings and other green matter in the compost heap. Tilled under in the fall, their humus-building qualities provide improved structure for all types of soil. (See "Fall rototilling.")

LETTUCE HINTS. Seed will germinate if just tossed on the ground (even frozen ground). Seed must be exposed to light and moisture for germination and need not be covered or — if so — very lightly with peat moss or straw. Some gardeners grow a special patch of head lettuce *to harvest like leaf lettuce.* Heads won't form, of course, with regular cutting — but leaves are tastier and more crisp than some leaf varieties. Spacing for leaf lettuce can vary, according to how you plan to harvest. If you pick outer leaves over a period of time, space 10 inches apart. If you intend to harvest the entire plant at once, spacing can be as close as four inches. When you harvest head lettuce, cut the head a few inches from the base rather than pulling up the plant by the roots. Some new leaves will form and they're tasty when young. For crisp texture, pick lettuce in the morning or late evening (ditto peas, chard and spinach). "Ruby" lettuce can be grown as a house plant if grown in a deep container (about 8") and given adequate light, water and fertilizer. A salad can be harvested about once every three weeks all winter. For protective shading and protection against birds try an inverted

"V"-shaped wire frame covered with cheesecloth over the lettuce row. Look into "slow bolt" varieties such as Summer Bibb, Hot Weather, Slobolt and others. Be sure not to overplant lettuce; thinnings can be used in early salads or transplanted. For a tempting weekly choice, mix seeds of different types of lettuce and plant concurrently in a "wide row" (see page 15 footnote) every week to 10 days.

LIMA BEANS will bear longer and produce better beans if given plenty of food and water while pods are forming. Bush limas do better in cool sections than pole varieties; both types require thoroughly-drained and warm soil before planting; the soft-skinned seeds easily rot in cold soil Fordhook 242 and Henderson are popular varieties. Also consider Dixie Butterpea, a 75-day lima described as "without question the finest, meatiest, most delicious bush lima bean."

LIME helps make more efficient use of fertilizer, neutralizes soil acidity, provides nutrients and improves soil in other ways. Soil test will determine need. Some crops such as lettuce, beets, kohlrabi, spinach and onion prefer a limed soil. Keep lime away from potatoes, however. Mix lime with wood ashes — sprinkle around onion, cabbage and beets to prevent damage by root maggots; this same mixture kills squash bugs when applied directly on them. See footnote on page 29.

LIVING MULCH. Watermelon vines have been used successfully as a living mulch for root crops such as salsify (oyster plant), carrots, parsnips and onions. For example, try planting root crops in rows eight feet apart early in the season (with onions and carrots in outer rows for easier harvest). Once ground warms up, plant watermelon half way between the rows. Vines fill the "middles," creating a thick, moisture-retentive mulch around the root crops. Using the same idea, use *leaf turnips* as a mulch for cucumber vines and between non-staked tomato vines (ripening fruit lies on turnip tops rather than soil). Tomato vines themselves also can provide a living mulch around beets.

LIZARDS AND SNAKES — the toy variety available in the dime store — spook birds who might go after your lettuce, Swiss chard, beets, etc. Place decoys in the open, perhaps on a board, so they're highly visible to birds approaching the area. (See "Canopies of nylon netting...")

LOCATION OF YOUR VEGETABLE GARDEN is almost as important as the condition of the soil. Ideally, as one MGCA member described it, a garden site should be "fertile, well-drained, free of stones and weeds, gentle southern slope (3° - 10°), good air circulation, full sun, no nearby trees, loamy soil with a pH reading between 6.0 and 6.8 — and close to the kitchen door." Very few gardeners have this "ideal" garden site, *but get as close to it as you can.* (See "Shade-tolerant vegetables.")

LOOK INTO *"LUFFA CYLINDRICA"* — also known as "dishcloth" or "rag" gourd. Immature 6" fruits are edible cooked like zucchini; mature foot-long fruits look like just what they are — sponges. Once dried, luffa fruits are useful for dishes, car washing or in the bath. In specialty shops, these unusual sponges sell for up to $5.00 apiece.

MANURE TEA — to a pail of water, add 2-3 fistfulls of packaged cow or sheep manure (if fresh not available) and about 1/4 cup of fish emulsion. Mix and apply regularly to all plants and along rows. Can't burn. Or, gather manure in an old tea towel, tie and suspend in garbage can filled with water/fish emulsion mixture. Dip as needed. Keep containers covered.

MATCHBOOKS — save 'em as a treat for your peppers and eggplants. Tear out the matches from several matchbooks and put them in the bottom of each transplant hole. These acid-loving plants like the sulfur, which also lowers pH of the soil. Powdered sulfur, aluminum sulphate or iron sulphate will give similar results.

MELONS need full sun and a rich, porous soil (pH 6 to 6.5). Use a low nitrogen fertilizer, but one high in phosphorus and potash. Hold back water when watermelons begin to ripen; this develops sweetness. Plant radishes among the vines as beetle repellent. Place a board underneath fruits to avoid rot; also see "Collect coffee cans."

MIDGET VEGETABLES — grow some of these in a separate child's garden (or set aside a special row in the family garden)...just for fun...or if space is mini. Ideal for containers. Tom Thumb head lettuce (try this in a window box with red petunias) is ideal for individual salad servings — whole, halved or quartered.

MISTAKES MOST OFTEN MADE BY BEGINNERS:

(1) Rushing the season — wait for the ground to warm up (tomatoes, for example, planted later will catch up and *pass* plants set out in cold soil).

(2) Planting too deep. Cover vegetable seeds only 3 or 4 times diameter.

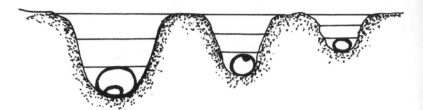

(3) Overfertilizing — this burns off the roots and sets back growth.

(4) Poor watering practices (see "Water").

(5) Selection of varieties not appropriate for locale — follow recommendations of local garden centers, extension services, state agricultural colleges, local MGCA chapters, etc.

(6) Too large a garden — 25' x 30' space is about right to feed a family of four.

(7) Sowing seed too thick (mix fine seed with sand first) — and, later, not thinning properly.

(8) Rough transplanting — root hairs are broken off or allowed to dry out.

(9) Lack of protection after transplanting — protect transplants against hot sun and wind for 2-3 days. Transplant on a cloudy day or in the evening. Many gardeners stick a shingle in the soil near the plant to provide this vital protection. Loose straw or hay mulch also works.

"MIX UP" YOUR PLANTINGS to confuse bugs or plant partial rows at different locations. Concentrations of one type of planting attract pests that attack that crop. Interplant marigolds, herbs.

MOLES OR GOPHERS A PROBLEM? To determine active tunnels, stamp all of them flat. Ones that reappear the next day are active. Check into commercially-available traps of various kinds or try these ideas:

1. Kleenex or rag soaked in peanut or olive oil and pushed into gopher or mole runways will chase the critters. Oil quickly becomes rancid and stinks 'em out.

2. Using the same principle, one gardener who had tried "everything else" finally got rid of moles with the help of two large dogs. Mole tunnels were dug open regularly and dog droppings dropped in. Moles took up residence elsewhere.

3. Vibration vexes moles. Stick a child's pinwheel in several spots around the garden if moles are a problem. A larger mole windmill ("Klippety-Klop") designed for this purpose is commercially available at garden centers (or write Lakeland Nurseries Sales, Hanover, Pa. 17331). See photograph above.

47

4. Plantings of scilla and castor bean also discourage moles and gophers (check poison warnings for castor bean if children in the area are as active as the moles). Or try this castor oil "recipe": whip two ounces castor oil to one ounce of liquid dish detergent in a blender to shaving cream consistency. Add water equal in volume to this mixture and whip again. Fill sprinkling can with warm water, add two tablespoons of castor oil formula, stir and apply to areas of heaviest investation (ideally after a rain or a good watering for deeper soil penetration).

5. Grub-invested soil attracts moles, so you can make your lawn less attractive to moles by eliminating grubs with milky spore disease (see "Japanese beetles"). (See "Quart-size pop bottles.")

MOTH BALLS are said to repel rabbits and bugs — but don't spread on soil. Hang small mesh bag of moth balls on trellises or fences, where beans, cucumbers, etc. are growing... or put moth balls in jar lids or similar shallow containers and place on ground (if children aren't apt to spot). (See "Bird bath.")

MOUND PLANTING — growing heat-loving plants such as tomatoes, peppers, squash and eggplant on enriched mounds of soil 10" high and 3' in diameter — encourages heavier rooting and better production. Works great with sweet potatoes, too, as they like a deep root run.

MULCHING TIPS. Gardeners everywhere give "mulch thanks" to mulch for the important benefits it provides. For example, a hay or straw mulch spread about 6-8 inches thick (settles to 2-3 inches) will: (1) prevent evaporation of water from the upper 6-8 inches of soil by as much as 70%; (2) stabilize soil temperature and keep roots cool (temperatures above 85° can stop root growth in many crops) and (3) prevent weeds from growing for about three months. In addition, organic mulch adds nutrients directly to the soil as it decomposes and, once turned under, improves soil structure (moisture and

nutrient-retention qualities of soil are improved; soil becomes more friable). Mulch prevents soil runoff, keeps vegetables cleaner and insulates crops from soil-borne diseases. And, of course, nature's most efficient soil builder — the earthworm — loves to burrow under mulch. *"Dos" and "don'ts" with mulching:*

- DON'T mulch a hot, dry soil. Wait until after a heavy rain or deep watering.

- DO use whatever is free, cheap or abundant locally — grass clippings, hay (salt marsh, fescue, prairie, etc.), straw (wheat, pine, etc.), bark, leaves (shredded, ideally), tobacco stems (but not around tomatoes), rice hulls, cotton burrs and hulls, pecan shells, peanut hulls, Spanish moss (reusable!), etc.

- DON'T overlook sources for free mulch in your own community. Manure mixed with sawdust, for example, is often available at stables for the asking. Ask around for sources for spoiled hay, often available free or at a reduced cost. (See "Trio of sources for free mulch.")

- DO apply a complete fertilizer high in nitrogen such as 10-6-4 or cottonseed meal BEFORE mulching with organic materials (avoid high-nitrogen ammonium nitrate, as it's getting a bad press). Organic mulches can cause a nitrogen deficiency as the mulch steals nitrogen from the soil as it decomposes. Try putting down a layer of partially-decomposed mulch or compost first, then apply the fresh organic mulch on top.

- DON'T go overboard with heavy mulches in a wet year, particularly if you have a heavy soil. A constantly soggy, heavy mulch restricts oxygen in the soil and encourages root fungus diseases.

- DO dry weeds out thoroughly before using as mulch. Never leave fresh-pulled weeds as a mulch on moist soil; many will sprout again. Oat straw and some other mulches tend to sprout. If they do, simply turn them over.

The type of mulch you choose allows you to control soil temperature and thus hasten maturity and raise yields. Many gardeners use organic mulches exclusively because of the important advantages outlined above. Others use a mixture of organic mulches and inorganic mulches such as clear, green and black plastic, aluminum foil, etc. — often covered with organic mulch. Advantages of different types:

- CLEAR PLASTIC heats up the soil early in the season by as much as 10% — but also stimulates weed growth. Water-filled plastic bags have worked well to warm up soil, such as for early corn or tomatoes.

- GREEN PLASTIC warms up the soil almost as well as the clear variety and does a better job stopping weeds.

- BLACK PLASTIC adds about 6% to soil warmth and eliminates all weeds. The plastics — white, green and particularly black — are useful around heat-loving plants such as melons, but most crops prefer a cool root environment.

- LIGHT BROWN PAPER MULCH WITH PLASTIC COATING (available commercially) *lowers* soil temperature as much as 8% and also keeps out weeds.

- ALUMINUM-COATED PLASTIC AND ALUMINUM FOIL decrease soil temperature about 10%. Both brown paper and aluminum foil mulches reflect the sun's rays.

- ORGANIC MULCHES, by far the most widely used, also keep the soil about 10% cooler and stop annual weeds if applied thick enough. In addition, growth-stimulating carbon dioxide is produced naturally by decomposing vegetation. *Organic mulches [except for sawdust] attract earthworms — miniature compost factories and one of the gardener's best friends. [To judge earthworm population, dig on a humid day a square of earth 7" deep and 1' square. You should find at least 10 wiggling friends busily creating humus.]*

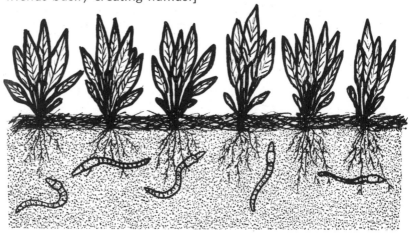

A to Z Mulching Guide

Mulching requirements for individual vegetables [and fruits] vary widely. Here's a brief A to Z mulching guide for individual crops [also see "Aluminum foil," Black plastic mulch," "Continuous year-round mulching," "Grass clippings," "Leaves" and "Living mulch"]:

ARTICHOKE. Use any nitrogen-rich mulch such as dry grass clippings. Use sparingly at first; increase mulch as season progresses. For winter harvest, mulch Jerusalem artichokes with a thick layer of leaves once soil has a frozen crust.

ASPARAGUS. Mulch heavily to prevent weeds during the growing season. For winter protection, use about 4" of hay, chopped leaves, leaf mold, straw, salt hay, ground corncobs, well-rotted manure or compost. In the spring, a loose hay mulch keeps the stump ends blanched and tender — plus prevents development of woodiness near the soil, making more of the asparagus spear edible.

BEANS. Since bean roots are close to the surface, heavy mulching will take care of weeds and eliminate the need for deep, extensive cultivation which could damage roots. Once good growth is underway, maintain a 4" straw, hay or grass clipping mulch.

BEETS. Apply light layer of grass clippings after planting to conserve moisture and prevent soil crusting. When sprouts appear, pull back this mulch to avoid damping-off problems. After thinning, apply more mulch and increase mulch gradually as growing season progresses. Hay or straw, tucked in close to the leaves, is recommended.

BLUEBERRIES. Mulch lightly when plants are first set out. As plants grow, increase mulch up to 6-8 inches. Use an acid mulch such as peat moss or pine needles.

BOYSENBERRIES. Heavy feeders, these like a mulch of well-rotted compost.

BROCCOLI. Mulch early with any non-acid organic mulch. Can stand a maximum of 4-6 inches of organic mulch.

BRUSSELS SPROUTS. See "Broccoli."

CABBAGE. Tuck partially-decomposed mulch up under the leaves after well established. This will slow growth somewhat, but they'll be

51

extra tender, green and succulent. Grass clippings, hay or sawdust are good.

CANTALOUPES. Use black plastic or thick, non-acid organic mulch (hay, straw, shells and hulls, grass clippings). Avoid sawdust and leaves. Mulch should be in place before fruit develops.

CARROTS. Use mulch very sparingly. When seeds are sown, very thin mulch of loose hay or dry grass clippings can prevent crusting of soil surface. Coffee grounds (mixed with a little ground limestone) can be used as mulch or side dressing.

CAULIFLOWER. See "Broccoli."

CELERY. Mulch deeply — almost to cover plants — to conserve moisture.

CHIVES. See "Onions."

CORN. Apply loose straw or hay mulch early to protect emerging sprouts from crows and other inquisitive birds. Once the corn is tall enough to shade the ground, mulch heavily (5-6") to conserve moisture and keep down weeds. Try hay, straw, dry grass clippings.

CUCUMBER. Thick mulches of loose chopped leaves, leaf mold, straw and hay are good. Mulch should be about 2 inches thick when settled; it should be airy, not compact. Put around plants when three inches high and before vines start to take off. Keep mulch 3-4 inches from stems.

EGGPLANT. Don't mulch until ground has warmed up and fruits are egg-size. Mulch should be deep enough to retard weed growth, but not too heavy, as eggplant likes it hot. Eggplant roots are shallow, so mulch also conserves needed moisture in the top two inches of soil where roots feed. To increase yield, put a 1-1/2 - 2' square of aluminum foil beneath each plant.

GARLIC. See "Onions."

KALE. See "Cabbage."

KOHLRABI. Thick, organic mulch maintains necessary moisture, boosts growth. Try hay or grass clippings.

LEEKS. See "Onions."

LETTUCE. When about 3-4" high, mulch with about 3" of straw or hay. Tuck up mulch under leaves for better growth, up to about 6-8" as the plant grows. Mulch means a cleaner harvest — no mud splatters. For an extra clean crop, mulch first with newspapers — then cover with straw or hay.

OKRA. Mulch heavily between the rows with well-rotted cow manure, old hay, straw or leaves. Apply only a light layer of mulch (try grass clippings) to the okra rows themselves — just enough to discourage weeds. Okra — like eggplant — needs a warm soil to produce well.

ONIONS. Mulching helps greatly by keeping down weeds, a "must" for good onions. Try chopped leaves or loose hay. Apply about 2-4" thick when tops reach 6-8". Leave bulb exposed to sunlight.

PARSLEY. Mulch heavily to conserve moisture.

PARSNIPS. Mulching prevents soil compaction. Any non-acid mulch will do. Once cold weather sets in, mulch heavily with leaves to protect crop from alternate freezes and thaws. This will extend harvest well into the winter.

PEANUTS. Mulch around plants should be heavy enough to keep soil from hardening; otherwise the plant growing tips (after flowering) cannot penetrate the ground where the peanuts form (during this period, keep soil moist).

PEAS. These like a cool, moist root run — so mulch early and heavily with a loose mulch like straw. Apply mulch lightly when seeds are sown, increase thickness as plants grow. Chopped or whole pea and bean vines provide a nitrogen-rich mulch for other plants (try these in your corn rows).

PEPPERS. Mulch after blossoming begins. Dark colored mulches such as leaf mold or cocoa bean hulls and peppers seem to go together. Hay mulch, on the other hand, stunts plants according to some tests. For extra-early peppers, place around each plant an 18" square of reusable black plastic or tar paper with about a 4-5" diameter circle cut out in the center.

POTATOES. Mulch heavily with oak leaves, straw, marsh hay or pine needles. If you grow potatoes below ground, hill plants before they begin to sprawl and then apply the mulch. You can grow potatoes above ground, right in the mulch, too. (See "Potatoes above ground?")

PUMPKINS. Mulch around each hill with rotted hay, composted leaves or straw. Before mulching, work in a manure feeding (dehydrated variety may be used). Sprinkle on some bone meal, too.

RADISHES. A light mulch is beneficial. Try chopped hay or loose straw.

RASPBERRIES. In tests sawdust and wood chip mulches have increased production by as much as 50%. Apply 3-4" thick at base of plants.

RHUBARB. Once the ground freezes, spread a heavy mulch of strawy manure or dried manure over the bed. Rake off in the spring to allow the ground to warm. Once sprouting begins, draw up a thick mulch. Straw or hay are good, but also try leaves or sawdust for the added acidity.

RUTABAGAS and TURNIPS. See "Beets."

SPINACH. After leaves have made a good growth, mulch heavily — about 3-4" — with grass clippings, chopped hay or ground corncobs. Avoid acidic mulches such as pine needles, leaves and sawdust.

SQUASH. Heavy mulch up to 4" is beneficial as weeding is difficult, particularly around vining winter squash. Compost and rotted sawdust are ideal, although any organic mulch will do. Leave the center open so that some heat can get to the middle of the plant.

STRAWBERRIES. May be mulched right after planting. Chopped hay or straw is the mulch most frequently recommended, but pine needles are more attractive (use 2-4" thickness). Sawdust also is popular. One benefit of mulch here is that it keeps the fruit clean. In the fall, spread compost around plants. Once ground freezes, maintain heavy mulch over winter, up to 6" of hay or straw.

SWEET POTATOES. Mulch heavily with compost, if available, as sweet potatoes are heavy feeders. On the sides of the rows, use old leaves, grass clippings, hay or straw.

SWISS CHARD. See "Spinach."

TOMATOES. A common mistake by many gardeners is mulching tomatoes *too early*. Heavy mulching when plants are first set out retards growth, as tomatoes need heat to start good growth. Best time is right after flowers appear or first fruit forms. Any organic mulch is fine. Wet grass clippings should be kept away from stems (see "Grass clippings"). Mulching during the growing season (6-8" of organic mulch) reduces fruit cracking and dry blossom-end rot and, if unstaked, mulch keeps sprawling fruit from rotting on the soil.

WATERMELON. Again, don't rush the mulch. Apply up to 6" of mulch after soil has been dampened thoroughly. Straw or hay are recommended. Draw mulch up to base of vine.

ZUCCHINI. See "Squash."

 AME YOUR PUMPKINS! Names can be added to a pumpkin by scratching name deeply (about 1/4") when pumpkin is about half formed.

NASTURTIUMS repel white flies, squash bugs, cucumber beetles and other pests around limas, melons and squash while they add color to the garden. Grow *climbing* variety with pole beans and cucumbers. Aphids in nasturtiums indicate lime deficiency in soil; dust with lime.

 AK LEAVES tilled under do not make the soil acid. This is an "old wives' tale."

OKRA, considered a southern vegetable, actually can be grown in Zones 3-10. Recommended spacing is generally 12-24", but tests in Arkansas have shown that an 8" spacing increases yields 25-35% when ample fertilizer and water are provided. Soak seeds 24 hours. Okra likes fish emulsion; feed 6-8 weeks after planting. Try interplanting cucumbers; they'll grow right up the big plants. Versatile and mineral-rich, okra can be boiled, broiled, fried, roasted or deep-fried, used in soups, stews and relishes, and preserved as pickles or frozen and dried.

ONION HINTS. If you prefer *more onion* and *less tops* for use as green onions, set onion *plant* very deep, with only 1/2 - 1" of green above ground (blanches 'em like celery). For bigger storage onions, grow from seed (in colder climates, start indoors or plant outside a month before average date of the

last spring frost). Also, if starting early inside, keep cutting back tops as they reach 3-4" to about 1-1/2 - 2" high. When choosing onion sets for planting, discard the largest — stick to those about dime size. Onion sets, incidentally, grow well just tossed on damp ground in early spring and covered with 6" of loose hay or straw. Or try planting onion sets *through* a newspaper mulch: moisten onion patch, spread 4 or 5 layers of newspaper over area (wetting each layer with a hose). Jam a hole through the wet paper with one finger and pop in a set. Firm well in moist soil. Cover newspapers with grass clippings, shredded leaves, etc. This method eliminates any potential problem with weeds, a particular problem with onions since stalks don't cast much of a shadow. If you grow onions from seed, check the catalogs for commercial varieties. They'll keep better. Keep onions watered and — most importantly — be sure bulbs get plenty of sunlight (*keep soil brushed away from bulb so that about 2/3 of bulb is above ground*). Keep after the weeds or yield will suffer. When plants are about 6-8" high, give a fertilizer boost. Interplant radishes as trap plant for onion root maggots. Onion "rings" are decorative and productive. Arrange alternating one-foot rows of sets and plants in a semi-circle design, with increasingly larger "rings." Grow beets, carrots, lettuce, Babyhead cabbage or low-growing marigolds between curving rows (where available, try seedtapes for ease in making curving rows).

ONION SETS. You'll save money be growing your own. Plant onion seeds rather thickly late in the season (about July in most areas) in an area where earlier crops have been harvested. Fertilize well. Dry small bulbs as you would regular onions (see Section 3). Store indoors until needed in spring.

ONION VARIETIES? There are a lot of good ones. For a continuous supply for all uses, try this suggested "mix": Ebenezer (scallions in late spring, cooking and other uses during summer, leftovers for storage); Red Burgundy (poor keepers, but unsurpassed for salads and hamburgers during summer and fall); Hybrid Sweet Spanish (slicing and cooking in fall and winter); Pacesetter Hybrid (excellent storage onion).

Specific varieties here are not as important as the idea of planting a "mix" of onions to meet specific needs.

ORGANIC SPRAY FOR GENERAL USE: Using a blender, add one quart water and grind or chop three large onions, one whole garlic clove and two tablespoons of cayenne pepper (substitute two pods of hot pepper if available). Stir in one tablespoon of dish detergent after mixing other ingredients in blender. Strain and spray (except on edible foliage). Bury leftover "mash" between rows. Some gardeners grind or cut up plug tobacco, then boil it with hot peppers to make a spray for squash.

 APER BAGS will protect ripening corn from frost (also birds and less wily raccoons). Place bags over ears after they're pollinated.

PARSLEY growing in a large, deep flower pot sunk into soil makes it easier to bring in for winter growth. Start in late June with four parsley seeds; thin to the best plant as it grows. Cut back when brought in. Try Curled Leaf.

PARSNIP HINTS: (1) Time planting at the right time for your area to provide a long, cool growing season; (2) Use fresh seed only; (3) Sow shallow, as seed has little "pushing up" power. Sow radish seed very thinly in the row to break the crust of earth, provide shade and mark the row; (4) Keep furrows moist, but not wet. Overwatering creates puddling, which promotes crusting; (5) Thin carefully when about 3" to stand the same distance apart. Check to be sure you leave *just one plant* in each spot (seedlings sometimes grow inter-

twined); (6) Water consistently throughout the long growing season. Not enough water creates dry, mealy roots; too much water will give you stringy, tasteless roots; (7) Cold weather sweetens the taste, so don't harvest until after at least the first few frosts. In many areas, parsnips can be harvested into the winter or — if protected by mulch — even early the following spring before weather warms up; (8) To preserve the distinctive taste of the parsnip, don't peel the roots.

PARTIAL ROW PLANTING of quick-maturing vegetables — a third every week or so — spreads the harvest and avoids waste. Extra easy with seedtapes: just get out the scissors. With *any* vegetable, never plant more at one time than you are likely to use at maturity. Don't make the common mistake of overplanting simply because "that's how many seeds were in the seed packet."

PEA HINTS. Biggest problem: you have to plant so many to get a big enough harvest. Most common mistakes: (1) planting single rows placed far apart and (2) late planting (peas go in as soon as you can walk in the garden in very early spring; they'll even withstand freezing). Plant early, midseason and late varieties at the same time (also see "Wando peas" and "Edible-podded peas"). Plant rows 6" apart on opposite sides of a fence or — for a huge yield — try "band" or "wide row" planting of low-growing varieties. Broadcast seeds about 2" apart in wide bands (up to 4' wide) in area in good tilth and with nitrogen fertilizer added. Walk on soil to plant (soil should not be wet). Add a little soil to planted area and level with the smooth side of a rake, then water. Plants will hold each other up. If you grow climbing varieties, try black plastic netting.

PEANUTS can be grown as far north as Ontario (use a *small seeded* variety in cold climates)...are decorative enough to be used as a vegetable garden border (try combining these with petunias)...and make a great fun crop for children. Protect from rabbits.

PEAS IN A PILLOWCASE. Shell peas fresh from the garden (no blanching, cooking) and place loose in a pillowcase closed with a "twistem." Plop pillowcase in the freezer. Peas freeze *individually* since they're dry. When you're ready for some, just dip in the pillowcase with a measuring cup. Use different colored pillowcases to separate varieties. Harvest too puny for a pillowcase? Substitute a plastic bag.

PEAT POTS, peat "cubes" and expandable pressed peat pellets used for starting seeds eliminate transplanting shock since roots aren't disturbed (particularly important for melons, cucumbers). Thoroughly soak; pinch out bottom; sink peat units *below* ground level. (See "Undisturbed root system.")

PEPPER HINTS. Transplants should be buried to top pair of leaves. Add compost or manure to planting hole. Grow peppers S-L-O-W with little or no nitrogen; sidedress once fruit sets. Hill up soil around base of stem gradually to give the stems added support when bearing the fruit. Try staking brittle pepper plants if production is extra heavy. . . or just snap a *peony ring* around the plant. (See photograph, page 33). When you cut peppers (never twist 'em off), leave a 1/2" stem. They'll keep better. (See "Matchbooks.")

PERMANENT ROW MARKERS. Seed packets stuck on a stick don't last very long. Instead, save aluminum pie pans and frozen food trays. Using scissors, cut labels to desired size. Place aluminum piece on a soft surface (such as several sheets of paper) and with a ball-point pen and a little pressure you can permanently emboss the plant name on the row marker. Make some oval-shaped tags, punch a hole in one end and you have a permanent identification tag for roses, shrubs, etc.

PERMANENT STRAWBERRY BED saves work, money. Plant June bearers or everbearers in rows spaced 8" apart and plants 3' apart in the row. Let first plant on each end of row make one runner down the row. Allow two of the earliest runners on all other plants to remain — one up and one down the row. These replace the original plant the second year. Thereafter, only single runners that develop from a plant here and there will be needed to maintain the bed. Replanting is eliminated. Production is continuous as little or no strength is taken away from the leaves to make runners.

PICK CROPS REGULARLY and they'll produce longer (peas, beans, broccoli, cucumbers, okra, acorn squash, zucchini, chard, tomatoes, peppers, New Zealand spinach, eggplant, etc.).

PICKLING FAILURE? Never soak pickles in water; they fill with water and can't soak up the brine. This is the reason for most pickle failures.

PLAN FIRST, THEN PLANT. Use a pencil when you *plan* your garden layout (in case you change your mind) AND when you *plant* (to make pre-spaced holes for beans, corn and other large seeds). Graph paper, with each square representing one foot, makes planning easier.

PLANT A PURPLE PATCH. Varieties are productive — plus pretty (particularly when interplanted with bright yellow marigolds). Start with the traditional ruby lettuce and deep purple eggplant...then expand your purple patch with purple cauliflower (turns green when cooked), purple Royalty Beans (can be planted earlier than traditional snap beans; also turns green when steamed for two minutes; shunned by the Mexican bean beetle), purple kohlrabi (somewhat later than white; colorful for salads), purple cabbage (try Ruby Ball or Red Rock) and, of course, burgundy onions.

PLANT PRUNING at the right time can work wonders for better fruit set. If cantaloupe vines have lots of foliage but few fruits setting, try pruning vines when they reach 4-5 feet. Remaining blooms then will set melons. Same idea works with watermelons, squash, tomatoes, gourds and other crops. After pruning, strength of plant is converted into fruit production. Removal of excess blossoms increases the size of remaining fruit. Pruning of any kind is particularly important late in the season; if too many blossoms set, developing fruits will not have time to mature.

PLANT TENTS. Commercially-available hotcaps are handy in early spring, but sometimes you'll wish you had giant-size ones to accommodate larger plants up to 15" tall. Make your own by mounting large-size plastic food storage bags over a "teepee" tent made of two wire coat hangers (cut hooks off, bend into shape, wire top together). Legs go into the ground for added stability; tuck up a little soil and then some mulch at the bottom. Other coat hangers can be stretched into foot-long pieces with a 6-inch "arm" on each end. Pushed into ground, these hold black plastic, newspaper and aluminum foil mulches securely.

PLASTIC "BUBBLES" commercially available to go over basement window wells to keep out leaves can double as a cold frame. Ventilate from inside. Lettuce could be grown during winter and harvested from inside. You can find lots of uses for such a handy device.

POLE BEANS — a dense row — planted along north side of tomato patch trap extra warmth for tomatoes and ward off chilling winds in early autumn.

POTATO BEETLES can be repelled by planting green beans near potatoes (in turn, the potatoes help keep Mexican bean beetles from attacking the beans).

POTATOES ABOVE GROUND?

Potatoes can be easily grown *above ground in a thick straw or hay mulch* and it's been done for over 20 years. Ideally, prepare the soil for this method the previous fall by spreading a 3" layer of leaves over the area (potatoes do best in an acid soil with pH of 5.0 to 5.5) after working in some manure or compost. Otherwise, fertilize in the spring (but never with fresh manure). When you're ready to plant, place potatoes every 12" in rows one foot apart *directly on the soil or on a 1" leaf mulch* (latter is preferable). Cover with a foot of straw or hay and *maintain this depth throughout the growing season* so soil and lower portion of mulch remain moist. Mulch cover keeps light out, too...so potatoes don't turn green. Keep area well watered. Vigorous plants will grow up through the mulch (but weeds won't); potatoes will form right in the mulch. Just "part" the mulch to harvest new potatoes without disturbing plants. Once the plants die down, harvest the main crop. This growing method seems to eliminate potato beetles and other pests. Close planting increases space efficiency by 40%. Potential problems of marauding mice and seed potatoes drying out can be eliminated by planting *shallowly*, with eyes just covered with soil — and mulching with 6" of partially-rotted leaves or straw or freshly-cut, partially-dried grass clippings (these mulches settle to 3"). Compared to unmulched plots, 1975 tests[*] show that use of an organic mulch and shallow planting greatly increased tuber production: grass clippings (40-89% increase); decayed leaf mulch (45-68% increase); straw (30% increase).

[*] Conducted by Organic Gardening and Farming Research and Development Group at New Organic Gardening Experimental Farm, Emmaus, Pa.

POTATO "EYES" — when you cut potatoes, cut as much potato as possible with each eye. Enough moisture then will be retained to sprout it even if soil is loose or dry. Cut only one eye to each set, NEVER OVER TWO (or you'll get only "mini" potatoes). Keep in mind that egg-size potatoes (which you may be tempted to plant whole) have as many eyes as their big brothers. And don't plant the tip end — the cluster of eyes it contains are too close together to produce vigorous plants. Always use certified seed potatoes — those grown under controlled conditions to be free of virus disease. Cut potatoes three or four days before planting and allow to dry enough to form a scab before too much sprouting takes place (the scab prevents the seed piece from rotting in extreme moisture). If you want only a small planting, check seed catalogs for certified precut potato sets ready for planting. You can usually buy a "mix" containing an early, middle and late variety — which lets you spread the harvest over a longer period.

PUMPKIN AND SQUASH WATERING TIP — Watering all along stalks will bring out the dark brown, hard-shelled squash bug, which then can be handpicked. Repel by planting radishes, marigolds.

"PUNK" — According to Mark Twain, a green watermelon says "pink" or "pank" when thumped with the knuckles. A ripe one says "punk." Or avoid the hassle with "Golden Midget"; it turns yellow when ripe.

QUART JARS or any wide-mouthed open container make effective traps for pesky, leaf-eating grasshoppers. Half-fill several with a 10% molasses/90% water solution and place where infestations seem worse. Preventive hint: As grasshoppers lay eggs in late summer (top 3" of soil), fall rototilling destroys egg clusters.

QUART-SIZE POP BOTTLES can be used to scare away rabbits (also moles). Fill half-full of water and bury upright or at an angle so that about 4" projects above ground. Place about every four feet around borders. Whistling noise of wind over the open top of the bottles frightens the critters. Standard-size soft-drink or beer bottles may be substituted.

QUIT WAITING FOR LARGE "END OF SEASON" HARVESTS if you're after top frozen quality. Freeze (or can) vegetables in small amounts — fresh picked each day — for best quality. Vegetables for freezing should be harvested when somewhat younger than desired for eating fresh. Beans, for example, are best before the beans inside the pods get plump. As you store packages in the freezer, "mix 'em up" for a ready access to a variety of vegetables (or you may be looking for corn buried under 30 pints of beans).

R ABBITS NIBBLING DOWN YOUR ROWS? Surest safeguard is a 30" fence of 1-1/2-inch mesh sunk 6" underground (24" above ground). Powdered rock phosphate, flour or talcum powder sprinkled on foliage of beans, tomato seedlings, etc. works for many. Success also has been reported with dried blood meal sprinkled on *soil* around plants [*but never directly on the foliage*]. Re-apply after a rain. Rabbits apparently panic at the odor. Not recommended: marigolds planted around garden *strictly* as rabbit deterrents. Many rabbits love to munch marigolds.

RACCOONS RAIDING YOUR CORN? Nothing seems to be absolutely foolproof, but gardeners have reported varying degrees of success with these "coon chasers":

1. Electric fencing — one of the best deterrents. First strand should be 6" above soil; the second about 15".

2. Host a "corn watch" slumber party at the corn patch — the grandchildren will enjoy the sleeping bag outing. Add a few dogs for good measure.

3. Leave a transistor radio on all night (protected by a plastic bag). Talk shows and rock 'n roll stations seem to work best.

4. Floodlight the garden during key corn ripening periods — flick the light on and off every now and then. Some gardeners place several blinking lanterns around the corn patch; others string up blinking outdoor Christmas lights around the borders.

5. Keep a brave dog tied nearby. Ideally a coon dog.

6. Grow pickling cucumbers, pumpkins, watermelon or winter

63

squash as living "fence" around perimeters. A coon likes to see around him and he may not want to enter the vine jungle. *Avoid gaps or he'll slip through. Once he's had a taste, nothing works!*

7. Grow at least a double row of a very late variety as a protective border around early sweet corn. Coon waits for the late variety to ripen (while you sneak in and get the early corn).

8. 3-4 foot fence of chicken wire with loose overhang of wire projecting above. Overhang needs to be about 1-1/2 - 2 feet. The coon's weight keeps him from climbing such a floppy arrangement.

9. "Corn cocoon" — wrap smaller corn patches in *black plastic netting;* stretch around sides and across top, anchor to ground.

10. Sprinkle *cayenne pepper* on ears and *lime* around borders.

11. Place dog droppings between the plants (*not* between the rows). Animal odors sometimes spook off a coon. Roaring success has been reported with *lion manure* (see "Circus in town?").

12. Walk *barefoot* around borders at dusk. Finally — never put off harvesting corn that's ready "until tomorrow." *The coon or coon family will invariably visit that very night!*

RADISHES do extra well and become tender if interplanted with lettuce. Even if you don't like radishes, plant 'em anyway all around the garden as "trap" plants for insects, who love radish tops, and for root maggots. They're a "must" around cucumbers and squash to repel cucumber beetle. Deep-

rooted Icicle radishes do a great job of breaking the soil for other root crops and all radishes are excellent for marking the rows of slower-maturing crops. And if you've been wanting to interest a child in vegetable gardening, a package of radish seeds will do it every time! (See "Watermelon-size radish.")

RAISED BEDS made of 2 X 8s and stakes (length optional) and no wider than four feet are ideal for carrots and other root crops (remove stones, lumps). For carrots, Nichols Garden Nursery suggests filling such a bed with 1/5 garden loam, 2/5 clean sand and 2/5 compost, well-rotted manure or peat moss. All ingredients should be mixed. Sprinkle bone meal on top, then rake down into a fine seed bed. Broadcast carrot seed, cover with 1/4 inch fine sifted peat moss. Water, and keep bed well moistened, but not soggy wet. Pull carrots as they are ready. You'll get carrots in fall if you sow seeds in July.

RAKE HANDLE tamped into soil lightly with your foot — short cut to making a seed furrow. For very short rows, try a yardstick (keep this handy to check space between rows and as a guide to keeping rows as close to parallel as possible).

RED AND ORANGE COLORS attract leafhoppers, flea beetles and other insects. As a trap, paint milk cartons bright orange-red and apply a light coat of Tanglefoot (available at garden centers). Set at 12-foot intervals in the garden. After a week or two, they'll be covered with insects. Discard; replace with new traps. (See "Yellow plastic dishpan.")

ROTATE CROPS whenever possible for fewer bug and disease problems (both can live over the coldest winter in the soil) and for better production. Rotation is particularly important for members of the cabbage family. Each crop takes something different from the soil — leaf crops consume nitrogen, root crops take potash from the soil. So switch leaf and root crops when you rotate. Try dividing your garden into quarters. What was in quarter Number 1 this year goes into quarter Number 2 next year, etc. Tests have shown that clockwise rotation produces larger, fuller growth than counter-clockwise rotation.

 ARAN WRAP or similar clear plastic anchored with rocks or boards and laid over just-planted seed bed speeds up germination by warming the soil and keeps: (1) the soil moist; (2) a crust from forming and (3) birds from eating the seed. Remove promptly as soon as seedlings show.

SCISSORS should be used to thin shallow-rooted seedlings such as onions. Normal thinning methods often pull up too many plants. Scissors also come in handy for cutting lettuce and spinach quickly.

SEED (GROWING YOUR OWN) — See "Varieties."

SEED STARTING HINTS. Soak larger seeds such as corn, squash, cucumber, melon, peas, pumpkin and eggplant...seeds with a hard crust such as parsley and celery... plus harder-to-germinate seeds such as carrots, turnips, beets and chard. Use warm tap water, rain water, a weak tea solution or a weak solution of liquid manure. Soak seeds for 24 hours — *but change water at least twice during this period or oxygen will be cut off and seeds will spoil.* Chill seeds of cold-loving plants such as spinach, peas (see "Ice Cubes") and lettuce in refrigerator for even faster germination. One spinach lover always chills seeds for one week between damp blotters. When sowing seeds, try to have top inch of soil especially rich in humus. When seeds are covered, firm the soil to give seeds intimate contact with moist (not wet) soil. In hard soils, make a "V" shaped furrow and fill with water, drain and fill in with loose soil, sand or vermiculite before sowing seeds. A good technique for larger seeds is to make a drill for seeds, soak these with water, press seeds into the wet soil and cover with barely moist soil. Top this off with *dry soil* on the surface — always a good practice as this encourages deep rooting. Early sowing tip: plant some seeds 2-3 weeks earlier than normal; if no germination occurs in 12 days, plant the seeds again. Nothing to lose, except a few seeds.

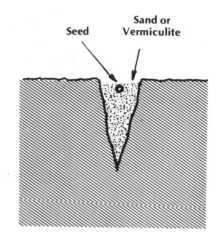

Seed / Sand or Vermiculite

- SOAK THE SOIL the day before you're planning to plant seeds or transplant; this is particularly beneficial in midsummer.

- HOT, DRY WEATHER — AND YOU WANT TO PLANT A FALL CROP? Plant seeds somewhat deeper than in the spring. To conserve moisture and prevent soil crusting, mulch newly planted seed rows with a 6" band of shredded peat moss or sawdust 1/2" thick; keep moist for at least a week. These extra steps can guarantee fall planting success.

SHADE-TOLERANT VEGETABLES include lettuce, spinach, parsley, cucumbers, bush beans, sweet potatoes, broccoli, Swiss chard, beets, cabbage, carrots, chives, kale, leeks, mustard, green onions, radishes and turnips. Some can be grown in pots and moved into the sun for short periods. Sunniest spots should be reserved for corn, tomatoes, pumpkin, squash, okra, eggplants, peppers and lima beans.

SHEEP MANURE COMPOST (dehydrated garden center variety) is better for vegetables than similarly-packaged cow manure. You can't use too much of this — lots of uses.

SHRED SPENT CORN STALKS before adding to compost heap to prevent corn borer from overwintering in stalks.

SLOPING PLOT? Run rows across the slope to minimize erosion, retain moisture. (See "Direction of rows.")

SLUGS A PROBLEM? Set out shallow pans or wide-mouthed jar tops of stale beer at ground level around the garden at night (but not where cats are apt to spot, or they'll lap it up). Slugs and snails love beer (they're after the yeast); they drown (perhaps dead drunk) by the droves. One teaspoon dried yeast with three ounces of water may be substituted;  this has attracted more slugs than beer in some tests — although beer has a good track record (one gardener trapped over 1,000 in three nights). If your slugs and snails are teetotalers, try grapefruit rinds (replacing after 2-3 days). Sprinkle slaked lime or wood ashes along rows; sprinkle slugs/snails with salt when you spot 'em (see "Bug traps"). If your garden is surrounded by lawn, try a barrier of sharp sand or cinders to keep out slugs. Oak leaf mulches apparently provide a "bitter atmosphere" which slugs can't stand. A large cabbage leaf inverted on the ground makes a good trap — as do boards. If coal ashes are available, line garden *paths* with 'em. Texture of coal ashes discourages slugs (they can't abide dry, powdery or sharp, prickly surfaces); when ashes decompose, they release sulfur which — combined with water — forms sulfuric acid (lethal to slugs). Powdered rock phosphate will deter slugs, plus enrich your soil. Toads thrive on 'em as a tasty treat.

SOAP — scratch a bar of soap before you go into the garden. Dirt under fingernails then washes out easily. Or just wear gloves.

SOFT ONIONS? Don't pitch 'em — plant 'em! As a California gardener reports: "These produced some of the finest green onions I ever ate."

SOIL-BUILDING TIPS. For compact, heavy soils, work into the soil (up to 1/3 the volume) compost mixed with sand or perlite. This allows drainage. Agricultural gypsum also is recommended for heavy clay soils

— simply spread and water in 25 pounds to each 500 square feet each year for several years. For loose, too sandy soil, add compost or manure along with peat moss — again up to 1/3 the volume. Replace compost and manure annually. Peat moss, although it has no direct nutritive value, remains in the soil for a long time and serves as a storehouse for water and fertilizer. From pure sand, you can create a productive soil quickly by digging out the bed two feet deep and laying roofing paper on the bottom. Put in a foot layer of organic matter, soil and fertilizer...then replace the sand and plant. The tarpaper holds the mass together until plants make sufficient fibrous roots to bind it. The paper then disintegrates.

SOWING TIP: Make furrows twice the planting depth specified; drop in the seed; half fill planted furrows with finely pulverized soil. As seedlings grow, wind and water will fill the furrow with soil. Plants benefit by having a deeper, firmer rooting.

SPACING TIP. Cultivation instructions on seed packets and in gardening books often assume machine cultivation. "Distance between rows" typically is much wider than needed for home garden cultivation. You'll often read "rows two feet apart" for peas, yet they grow nicely on each side of a fence (about 6" apart). In fertile, humus-rich soil, plants can be spaced much closer than normally indicated, too. Experiment to determine the closest spacing for each crop under your own conditions.

SPINACH, an easy-to-grow vegetable, is a favorite for many. Once you've harvested the first crop, try sowing another in a row where early peas grew. The nitrogen in the soil provided by the peas benefits the spinach, which should mature before summer heat hits. To extend the "spinach" season even further, try one of these spinach substitutes (and, if you're a real spinach fan, plan on a late sowing of regular spinach for fall maturity) (See "Harvesting hints," Section 3):

> • NEW ZEALAND — although not a true spinach, it tastes so much like spinach that it is called by the same name and is grouped with spinach in the seed catalogs. Seeds have a very hard case; soaking them or cutting a notch in the seed case with the edge of a small file will hasten germination. Water well until sprouting takes place. Plant sparingly, as one plant often covers a 3-4 foot square space. Stands heat well — can be picked repeatedly all summer and fall. Often reseeds itself for a bonus crop year after year. Sow seeds 1- 1-1/2" deep after danger of frost is past.

> • MALABAR — Noticeably more "spinachy" in taste than New

Zealand, Malabar is another hot-weather substitute for spinach. Produces an abundance of bright, glossy leaves on long, viney stems. Grow it on a fence or trellis to save space (grows 3-5 feet). Like New Zealand (and Swiss chard), Malabar is a "cut and come again" vegetable.

SQUASH BORER DAMAGE? (1) Locate borer by splitting stem near wilt, fish out borer with wire; (2) mound soil over joint beyond borer damage (cover about two feet of vine). Water well. This action permits the vine to put down new roots. Preventive care tips: (1) try throwing a handful of soil over each runner at two or three leaf nodes as the plant grows; (2) squash borer along with related insects can be eliminated from summer and winter squash as well as cantaloupe by soaking the seed of these garden favorites in *kerosene* overnight. You don't believe it? Plant one hill of seed NOT soaked in kerosene and see the difference. This idea has been successfully used for over 20 years.

SQUASH BUDS harvested just before they open into blossoms are delicious washed and sautéed in butter.

"SQUEEZE TEST" for soil (to determine if it's too wet to work): Squeeze a handful of soil, then poke it with your finger. If it sticks together, it's too wet. If it crumbles, get growing!

STAGGER ROWS TO CONSERVE SPACE, INCREASE YIELDS. Arrows below represent the minimum spacing between plants. The same crop can go in the "middles" or you can use this bonus space for intercropping other crops.

THIS...   **INSTEAD OF THIS...**

START SMALL if you're a first-time vegetable gardener. Too large a garden the first year can make you soon want to throw in the trowel.

STERILIZING SOIL. See "X-tra potent soil for transplants."

STORAGE HINTS. See Section 3 beginning on page 92.

STRAWBERRIES. See "Circular, three-tiered pyramid beds" and "Permanent strawberry bed."

STRAW-GROWN CARROTS. For a late summer crop, try this tip from a Nebraska gardener: spread straw over the ground and cover with a thin layer of soil (with a little dehydrated compost mixed in). Broadcast carrot seeds over the entire area, then cover with another thin layer of soil/compost.

SUMMER SQUASH is often overplanted. One or two plants is sufficient for most families. When the first planting of zucchini starts to bear, plant another hill or two to spread the harvest. Give lots of room.

SUNNY BORDERS? Lawn perimeters can be converted to "mini gardens." Eat your landscaping! Try "triangular" plantings of corn (three stalks) in corners of garden, or grow several rows against a fence, as shown here.

SUPPLEMENTARY FEEDING IS IMPORTANT: (1) when flowers are forming on tomatoes, peppers, eggplants, melons and squash and (2) when root crops are beginning to form good, mature roots.

SWISS CHARD — try this "cut and come again" vegetable if you're not already a fan. Unlike spinach, it thrives in summer heat and produces all summer. See special harvesting tips in Section 3. Chard offers a triple dividend: (1) thinnings are tasty in early spring salads; (2) leaves are cooked like spinach or mustard greens; (3) stalks are cooked and served like asparagus. Fordhook Giant is a popular variety. Rhubarb Swiss chard, somewhat sweeter, has green leaves with red stalks and ribs and will be the prettiest vegetable in your patch. Many vote it best in taste, too. *And you and your company will enjoy...*

SWISS CHARD PIE (special for the ladies). You'll need 1 small onion, 1/2 cup butter, 30 leaves torn into bite-sized pieces (discard stalk — or cook later), 2 eggs, 1/2 cup grated cheese (optional). Using a frying pan with lid, sauté onion in butter. Once onion is transparent, add chard to pan with little or no additional heat and leave until chard wilts (about a minute or two). Coat leaves with butter until all leaves are covered. Put in pie plate and break eggs on top and spread with fork. Add topping of cheese. Bake at 350 degrees until egg is firm. A real winner!

ARPAPER COLLARS (available at garden centers) around the stems of root crops keep the flies that deposit eggs of root maggots from doing their thing.

"TEEPEES" TUMBLING? If you've had trouble with bamboo or wooden stake pole bean "teepees" being blown over in a strong wind, try the "Southern Florida way" of bracing them. Set heavier, individual posts approximately 10-12 feet apart in the row and run a heavy wire between posts. Secure "teepees" to this anchor wire.

THIN PLANTS to recommended spacing while about 3" high and while soil is moist. "Musts" for early thinning are strong-germinating vegetables such as lettuce, radishes, beets, sweet corn, carrots, turnips and spinach. Toss thinnings from the spinach row into spring salads along with the thinnings of lettuce, beets and chard.

TOAD HOUSES (clay flower pots turned upside down with hole punched in side) and pan of water nearby will encourage toads to stay. Each will eat about 10,000 insects in three months . . . plus lots of slugs.

TOBACCO IS TABOO. Because of tobacco mosaic virus, smoking in the garden can be hazardous to the health of tomatoes, peppers, eggplants and even petunias. If you smoke, scrub hands with soap and water before handling these plants. (Smoking, too, is dangerous around straw or hay mulched garden. Don't cause a flowering inferno.)

TOMATO FRUIT SET can sometimes be increased by either shaking the vine or hitting the top of the stake to which the plant is tied. Best time to do this is in the middle of a warm, sunny day. Many successfully use commercially-available "blossom-set" hormone sprays. *Chilling* seedlings when about 1 - 1-1/2" tall (after first true leaves have appeared) for 2-3 weeks at 50° - 55° (night temperature) increases the number of ultimate flowers, results in larger fruit clusters and gives *earlier yields.*

TOMATOES ALL WINTER? Look into *Pixie* — see "Zero weather."

Indoor-outdoor Pixie Hybrid

Illustrator Robert Fischer's garden

TOMATO PRUNING AND STAKING TIPS. Bushy, low-growing *determinate* tomatoes, which include most of the early varieties, don't need staking or pruning. Pruning can reduce fruit yield considerably. *Indeterminate* varieties have stems that grow indefinitely and are the late varieties. These respond well to staking, training and pruning. There are also some *semi-determinate* varieties, with characteristics of both determinate and indeterminate — but most are of the two basic types. *Know what type of tomato you are growing!*

• TO STAKE OR NOT TO STAKE IS OFTEN THE QUESTION. Consider these findings from a scientific study:

1. Pruning and staking decrease total yields.

2. Twice as many trained plants than untrained plants can go into a given area (a healthy, sprawling indeterminate variety such as *Better Boy VFM* can take up to 16 or so square feet of space).

72

3. Staking results in cleaner fruit, less rotting and less insect and slug damage. (Mulching decreases damage for plants allowed to sprawl.)

4. Staking makes cultivation and harvesting easier, keeps the fruit clean and, because the plants get more light and air, enables the plants to better resist disease.

5. Trained vines give more uniform sized fruit, not much larger than untrained, but with fewer small tomatoes.

6. Trained vines take more time and labor.

7. Pruning has no significant effect on the rate of ripening.

8. There are more losses of fruit from cracking, blossom-end rot and sunscald on staked than on unstaked plants.

- IF YOU STAKE TOMATOES, YOU'LL WANT TO PRUNE THEM, TOO. There are three basic types of pruning — single-stem, double-stem and multiple-stem.

  SINGLE-STEM. Take off all shoots from the main stem. Suckers (shoots growing in the axils of the leaves) are removed when small. Prune once a week or sucker shoots will grow woody. Cut off lower branches as they turn yellow or brown. All pruning should be flush with the stem. Giant tomatoes, but fewer in number, can be produced with this method — but sunscald and cracking can be a problem.

  DOUBLE-STEM. Remove all except the first sucker immediately below the first flower cluster; this first sucker then is permitted to develop into a second stem. Both stems are tied to the same stake and all subsequent suckers are removed from both stems. Better production than single-stem pruning — fewer losses from sunscald and cracking.

  MULTIPLE-STEM. Compromise between pruning/training and natural growth. Select three or four good main stems to remain; pinch off all other branches. Although more tedious to maintain, this method produces more fruit than the more severe single-stem or double-stem methods. Because more foliage remains, the danger of cracking and sunscald is reduced.

- Leaving more leaves on a tomato vine increases photosynthesis, the production of sugar and starch. If you do prune tomatoes, *remove the center leaf only of the sucker BELOW a bloom or fruit cluster.* This stops growth of the sucker outward, but leaves the side leaves to absorb sun rays for increased photosynthesis. Take out all other suckers (grasp sucker between thumb and forefinger, bend one way, then break off the sucker in the opposite direction). If suckers are allowed to grow, a traditionally-staked and ade-quately-nourished plant will get too heavy with foliage and fruit and weight of the plant will pull over the stake.

- Here's a special pruning technique demonstrated at a MGCA vegetable growing seminar: Let each side shoot grow out to the first clump of tomatoes, then prune everything off beyond that and take out side shoots which originate below the tomato cluster on that individual side shoot. Then, when the cluster begins to get heavy, tie the cluster to the stake. (See "Tomato tying trick.")

- Plant *suckers* for a bonus "second season" (can be done up to July 15 in most areas). Have soil prepared (see below) and hole dug *before* cutting suckers, as you'll want to plant these right away. Ideally, do this on a cloudy day and late in the evening. Select suckers at least 8" in length and cut carefully from the mother plant. Remove bottom sets of leaves (usually one or two) and trim back the remainder one-half. Plant at least 4" deep in

74

pre-prepared pocket of sand and compost or "Tomato Soil" (see "Damping off a problem?"). Give a good soaking; keep soil moist for at least three days. Shield from sun for 2-3 days to prevent setback (try a large, inverted flower pot or basket). You'll probably lose a few, but most will take root.

- No pruning, staking or tying is necessary when you grow tomatoes in a 5' wire cylinder or cage — one plant per cylinder. This highly-successful technique, growing rapidly in popularity, is explained fully under "X-traordinary tomato production."

- If you stake tomatoes, always place stake at time of planting to avoid later injury to roots or any buried stem. Also, place stake on downwind side of the plant to provide support and lessen stress on ties.

TOMATO SEEDLINGS can be set in a 1" round hole cut out of the center of a seed potato instead of a peat pot. Add soil and tamp so each tomato stem stands upright. Place tomato-potato "grafts" on shallow pan containing 1" of soil. Tomato roots develop and grow right through the potato. Dig hole about a foot deep, add a shovelful of compost, then place "graft" on top. Cover tomato up to first leaves. Try a few of these for fun — plus a double yield from the same garden space.

TOMATO SPRAY FOR ROSES. Experiments have shown that tomatoes grown near or among roses have consistently eliminated black spot on the roses. Solanine, contained in tomato leaves, is a volatile alkaloid formerly used as an agricultural insecticide. . . but it apparently works as a fungicide, too. For equivalent protection, use a black spot spray: (1) grind up tomato leaves with a little water in blender; (2) to one pint of this solanine solution, add five pints of water and one ounce of corn starch. Keep solution refrigerated; (3) spray roses once a week. Try this. It works!

TOMATO TYING TRICK: Using a soft material (strips of an old sheet, old nylon stockings), make a single loose loop around the stem and cross the ends and make a tight tie with a double loop and a firm knot around the stake. This "figure-eight loop" leaves room for the stem to move with the wind and weight of the fruits, yet securely anchors the stem to the stake. Always tie plants so that fruits are away from stake.

TOMATO VOLUNTEERS COMING UP EVERYWHERE? Transplant these among early maturing crops such as peas or lettuce. Such "orphans" often are extra vigorous and can provide a bonus late crop for canning.

TOOL TIP. Handles of small garden tools can be painted red or another bright color. Harder to lose in the garden that way.

TOP 10 VEGETABLES grown by home gardeners, according to a leading seed company, are (in order of preference): tomatoes, beans, sweet corn, cucumbers, peas, lettuce, radishes, summer squash, melons and beets. *What happened to onions...or carrots...or peppers?*

TRIO OF SOURCES FOR FREE MULCH: Many utility companies shred tree trimmings and piles of the shredded material are often available for the hauling. If you live near a brewery, ask about the availability of spent hops. Sanitation departments often collect truck-loads of leaves off city streets via a suction pump; find out if some can be dropped off at your house instead of a landfill. Many cities welcome such requests.

UNDERSTANDING THE "BASICS" of vegetable culture requires more than scanning a seed packet. Buy a vegetable growing guide for instant in-the-garden reference...study library books during off seasons...ask questions...learn from your own mistakes. Spend some time with seed catalogs for cultivation instructions, new varieties and a roundup of useful garden aids that may not be available locally. Write MGCA (see page 2) for a full list of seed catalog suppliers. Time-saving tip: print or type a "prototype" catalog request letter and make copies as needed year after year. Drop 'em in the mail by Thanksgiving.

UNDISTURBED ROOT SYSTEM FOR TRANSPLANTS can be assured by this idea from a MGCA member in Kansas City: Cut styrofoam cups in half *lengthwise*, leaving the sides attached to the bottom and lower sides and secure the top with a rubber band. Fill with soil and plant seedling. When ready to plant, simply remove rubber band, spread the sides and pop happy plant in its new home. (See "Peat pots.")

UNFINISHED COMPOST, typically that on the top of the pile, is ideal for spreading as an initial "mulch" around tomatoes and other crops.

UNUSED SEED will keep longer if: (1) seed packets are sealed airtight in small plastic bags; (2) bags are placed in a coffee can with plastic lid;

(3) seed container is stored in a *cool*, dry place (heat destroys germination)*. Test germination percentage the next spring by "starting" 10 or so seeds in a wet, rolled-up paper towel, which then is enclosed with a damp, rolled-up terry-cloth dish towel. Put the "seed doll" in a clear plastic bag and seal; set in a warm spot. Seed should germinate in about 4-10 days.

UPSIDE-DOWN SEEDS A PROBLEM? Some say "eye" of bean seed must always be down; others say it doesn't matter. Roots naturally grow downward; leaves upward (process known as "geotropism") — so it's probably not worth the extra trouble.

UTILIZE SHAPES OTHER THAN SQUARES OR RECTANGLES occasionally for a more distinctive garden. Try a mixed vegetable-flower border in a gentle curve on one or two sides — particularly important if your garden is located within close proximity of your home.

ACUUM CLEANER IN THE GARDEN? Some gardeners use 'em to suck up white flies, flea beetles and aphids (plus dandelion heads). Battery-operated vacuums designed for cars work well, too. After regular house use, many gardeners empty lint bags into the compost heap rather than discarding.

* For 3-5 year seed storage, the National Garden Bureau suggests wrapping about two tablespoons of powdered milk in a facial tissue [held together with a rubber band] and placing this along with the seed packets in a dry, wide-mouthed quart jar with screw top. Store in refrigerator; don't allow long exposure to air when removing seed packets. Dried milk acts as a disiccant, drawing moisture from the air in the jar.

VARIETIES that are highly-productive and disease-resistant can be developed "in your own backyard" if you grow your own seeds. Check your library's gardening books for detailed instructions on specific crops. Here are a few basic tips — plus some pitfalls to avoid:

- Goal is to choose *only a few* outstandingly healthy, well-balanced plants by observation during the growing season with seed selection in mind. Label plants carefully (with string or piece of cloth).

- Base choices on *specific characteristics* you want to encourage. The first nice spinach plants that go to seed, for example, are the very ones you don't want. Pick the spinach plant that produces the longest and goes to seed *last*. Early fruiting or rooting will be the most desirable characteristic of other crops, such as broccoli, tomatoes or radishes.

- NEVER SAVE THE SEED OF HYBRID VARIETIES, as these are the result of cross-breeding of two pure-strain varieties and seeds saved will revert to the parent varieties. Seed may not be fertile (as with hybrid corn) and typically produces an "oddball" crop that probably won't be usable. . . one that is not true to either of the parent varieties.

- Plant only *one variety* of any vegetable you wish to seed. Many vegetables will crossbreed. Sweet corn will cross with field corn (see "Corn hints"). Don't plant beets near sugar beets or chard. Many gardeners plant early, middle and late varieties with different maturity dates (and pollination periods) — but this is "chancy" if you're planning to save seed. Other easily crosspollinated vegetables: Brussels sprouts, collards, kale, onion, radishes, kohlrabi, turnips — and members of the gourd family.* (Carrots, eggplant, tomatoes, pepper and celery are less easily crossbred; lettuce, okra, peas and beans are usually selfpollinated.)

   *A study of the gourd family (*Cucurbitaceae*) by a botanist shows that although *varieties* of the same species cross freely, the ONLY crossing that occurs *between species* in this family is in the genus *Cucurbita* (pumpkins, summer and winter squash, certain gourds). Not all species will cross even within this genus. "Acorn" squash, for example, will cross with "Butternut" but not with "Hubbard."

78

CUCUMBERS, ALTHOUGH IN THE GOURD FAMILY, DO NOT BELONG TO THE CROSS-CRAZY CUCURBITA GENUS. Varieties of cucumbers WILL cross with one another — BUT DON'T BELIEVE THOSE STORIES ABOUT CUCUMBERS CROSSING WITH CANTALOUPES, WATERMELONS, PUMPKINS, SQUASH, ETC. It simply does *not* happen.

- Let seeds ripen in the garden; bring in whole plant and place in dry place until pods are brittle and seed comes out easily. Sift out shaft with wire screening.

- Store seed in a dry, cool place — covered, but *not* in an airtight container. Stir seed frequently, removing any spoiled seed. Test seed for fertility (see "Unused seed") well in advance of planting time so you can buy more if necessary.

VERMICULITE, perlite, peat moss or prepackaged manure compost — place in furrow and sprinkle on seeds to aid germination (particularly useful if clods are a problem).

VERTICAL GARDENING saves valuable space and increases yields. Given full sun, one foot of vertical space will yield as much as the ten-times-larger area needed if vining crops are allowed to sprawl. If a fence or trellis isn't available, stretch a 12-foot or so length of concrete reinforcing wire between posts. This is heavy enough to train icebox-size Sugar Baby watermelons or cantaloupes to climb vertically (see " Cantaloupe sling"). On the same fence, you can interplant tomatoes, cucumbers, pole green beans, pole limas, red or green  Malabar spinach, Scarlet Runner Beans and, for crop protection, climbing nasturtiums. If you don't plan to grow the heavier melons, reusable black plastic garden netting (recommended over string type) can be substituted. Vining winter squash can be trained on "teepees" of three bamboo stakes (ditto tomatoes, beans). Try planting several pole beans next to corn stalks after corn is 6" high (this doesn't work as well with sunflowers because of light and root interference). If you're putting up a rabbit fence, at the corners — instead of a small stake — put up 6-7' stakes and let cucumbers or other crops climb up each stake. Similar in concept to the "cucumber tree" (see "Cucumber hints") is an idea used by a California MGCA member: He drives an 8-10' post in the ground and around this places a 10-15' *circle* of 5' high concrete reinforcing wire. Twine (about 15-20 lengths) connects the top of the wire to the top of the post. Pole beans are planted just outside the circle and grow to the tip of the post "teepee" fashion. (See "Wooden steel cable spools.")

VINES of various types (cucumbers, squash, gourd) can quickly disguise a compost heap. Leaf cover of vine helps to keep pile moist, too (or try a thick top layer of straw, hay or leaves).

WAGON OR CARRIAGE WHEEL can become a decorative, sectionalized herb "planter" — or these can be used to grow different varieties of lettuce. For easier cultivation, less stooping and better appearance, raise one or two bricks high. Use small wagon wheels for miniature roses. Or you can create a "wagon wheel" effect by growing herbs, lettuce, etc. in pie-shaped wedges forming a circle. Parsley, thyme, basil and similar smaller herbs also do well in a portable strawberry jar (pinch back as necessary).

WALKING ON SOIL compacts it in the early spring, so when sowing seed, lay a 2 X 6 board alongside the row you're about to plant — and walk the plank instead.

WALNUT (BLACK) TREES are notoriously allelopathic (harmful to other plants because of toxic secretions from roots). They're especially bad news for tomatoes, beans and peas growing nearby.

WANDO PEAS are heat-resistant and thus can extend growing season into summer. These also yield well if planted to mature in cool fall weather. If planting any variety of pea later than normal, plant seeds 1/2 inch deeper than recommended for early spring sowing — and be sure to mulch early and heavily. (See "Mulching tips.")

WARM UP THE GROUND EARLY for tomato, pepper and eggplant plants. Two weeks before planting, dig hole 15-24" deep and 1' wide. . . fill with water, add 1/4 cup of fish emulsion and drain. Ideally, repeat draining process two more times. A couple of shovelfuls of manure or compost goes on the bottom, with a little bone meal and a handful of superphosphate or rock phosphate stirred in. Grass clippings (first cutting in spring is richest in nitrogen) can be added to manure/compost mixture at bottom of hole. This "mix" will heat up and prompt earlier and more vigorous growth. Replace the soil until ground is level. Transplant roots should be *above* decomposing material.

WARM WATER is preferred by cucumbers. Set out a pail of water to warm up in the sun OR — if your hose has been out in the sun — water your cucumbers first. Water at 90° speeds up growth of ALL crops.

WATER — *an inch of water is needed each week when there is no rain.* Some vegetables are composed of 75-96% water, so it's important that plants not suffer a setback for lack of water. Water thoroughly, *regularly* and infrequently. Irregular watering causes irregular growth (and can even cause cabbage to crack). Water deeply as needed, then don't water again until the soil is almost dry. Frequent shallow watering does more harm than good. Ground level watering is best. Try "trickle system" with porous, "soil soaker" hose along row (tuck under mulch). Water in the morning in spring and fall and in the evening during summer (but early enough for foliage to dry). If drainage is a problem, dig a few drainage ditches. Some California gardeners surround gardens with elevated dikes to avoid run-off during irrigation. Heavy mulching to conserve moisture is a "must" in California and other areas with little or no rain from February to October. Newest innovation in watering is drip irrigation, developed in Israel, which provides root zone moisture between saturation and field capacity throughout the growing season. Moisture stress is eliminated and vegetable yields have been increased 30-100%. Check seed catalogs for drip and other new systems, such as water-saving, directional sprinkler "spikes" hammered into plastic hoses.

WATERMELON-SIZE RADISH. You'll want to check seed catalogs for the Sakurajima radish, which can weigh in at 15 or more pounds. Excellent flavor. Slip a seed or two in a child's garden and watch his or her eyes pop!

WEEDS can cut garden production in half! Cut or pull *early* (when before 2" high) and definitely *before* they go to seed. "One year's seeding makes seven years' weeding." Keep in mind that broadcasting manure over the entire garden can create a weed problem. Tests show that 40 pounds of weed seeds are contained in the average 25' X 25' garden plot — heavy mulch will help to keep 'em down under. Any that break through can be broken down via your compost heap — dandelions can help it heat up fast. (See "Mulching tips.")

WHITE GERANIUMS planted around garden attract and stun Japanese beetles. The crawly critters then are easy to collect and destroy.

WINTER SQUASH AND PUMPKIN don't *have* to take a lot of space. Look into the newer BUSH varieties. Golden Nugget squash grows on a bush, takes little space and has the flavor of Buttercup. Keeps well, too. Bush Acorn and Table King are bush varieties of the popular acorn squash. And check your catalogs for Cinderella pumpkin, which grows on a zucchini-size bush. Vining squash can follow peas up a trellis.

WIRE COVERS made from 3' wire fencing with 2 X 4-inch mesh and shaped into a tent are portable and can be used to keep birds away from peas, lettuce, strawberries and other crops. Covered at night with plastic, burlap or newspaper, they can double as frost protection or as cold frames. If available, substitute metal corn crib ventilators. (See "Canopies of nylon netting.")

WOODCHUCK OR GROUND HOG DAMAGE to sweet corn often is mistaken for racoon damage. Key differences: (1) woodchucks attack corn at any stage; coons wait until it's "just right" for picking; (2) coons strike only at night; woodchucks come early in the morning and early evening before dark; (3) woodchucks also devour nearby vegetables, such as bush snap beans and, their favorite, soy beans; coon damage normally is restricted to the corn patch. Fencing won't keep woodchucks out, as they're excellent climbers. Best bet recommended by an extension bureau expert: find their burrow (a new one typically is made each year and most have only one entrance); put several tablespoons of carbon disulfide (readily available in drug stores) on a rag; stuff treated rag at least a foot into burrow with a stick; cover hole quickly with rock or log and soil. Killing gas will form quickly. Several gas cartridges of the type available in garden centers also may be used. *The New York Times Book of Vegetable Gardening* reports that woodchucks will not cross a foot-wide strip of black plastic mulch placed around garden perimeters.

WOOD TOOTHPICK WATERING TEST for container-grown vegetables or flowers: Push toothpick into soil and pull it out. If soil clings, no water is needed. If it comes out clean, it's time to water again.

WOODEN STEEL CABLE SPOOLS — available free from some construction firms and often used for picnic tables — make dandy devices for growing cucumbers and pole beans. Hammer nails every 3 inches around base and top, insert tall pole into hole in top. Connect string from base, to top, then to tip of pole. Plant seeds around circular base; vines cover entire space. Ever seen a green May Pole?

X-TRA LARGE PUMPKINS can be grown by removing all the blossoms or young fruit except for one... never letting them run dry...and fertilizing once a week. "Big Max" is one variety that produces the 100-150 pound Jack-o'-lantern giants. For eating, try Baby Sugar, just the right size for a pie. (See "Name your pumpkins!" and "Winter squash and pumpkin.")

X-TRAORDINARY TOMATO PRODUCTION (about 150-200 tomatoes per plant) can be attained by growing a Better Boy VFN* plant inside a ring (18" diameter) of 5' concrete reinforcing wire. No pruning, no staking. Plant grows naturally...like a tree. Height is usually around 7 feet. Most fruits are 1-1/2 pounds or over. Also: try growing your tomatoes in a mixture of garden loam and one of the specialized tomato "soils." In the author's 1974 garden, a 33' row of just eight plants (3' between 18" diameter rings) produced over 1,400 tomatoes — many over two pounds. See photographs on pages 7, 33 and 116.

- Allow 3-5 feet between plants — remember, you'll need a *lot fewer plants* for same production. (Early maturing crops such as lettuce, spinach and peas can be planted between rings.)

- Prepare planting hole in advance according to "warm-up" technique described under "Warm up the ground early" (page 80).

* This hybrid variety has given consistent excellent results, but any indeterminate [see page 72], vigorous-growing tomato variety may be substituted.

- Since hole thus **prepared is** not the normal "cold soil," a 12" tomato plant can be planted *upright* (no need to bury stem on side) and *very* deep (leave only *top pair* of leaves above soil; pick off all others). Roots will grow all along this stem for added vigor. For later root watering, sink 2-lb. coffee can with holes punched in bottom about 8" from plant — fill with compost or manure. Add ring and watering can at time of planting.

- Ring can be covered with plastic film for frost protection.

- Rings: If you want all rings the same size, allow 5' 3" of concrete reinforcing wire with 6" mesh for each ring. Count 10 squares (5 feet), cut next 6" section in half. Bend and crimp this 3" extension to form ring; cut off other 3". Repeat process. (Note: If storage is a problem, make second ring 5-1/2', third ring 6' and repeat process for every three rings. Rings then can be "nestled" for storage.) One-size rings:

|---- 5' ----+-- 3" --| |---- 5' ----+-- 3" --| |---- 5' ----+-- 3" --|

- If rings are located in windy location, secure with a 6-7 foot stake plunged 1 foot into ground. You also can cut out cross wires at bottom, to create 6" spikes around rings, as shown above.

- Once plant begins to grow, do not sucker or prune in any way. Tying is not needed, of course. Branches may be trained inside ring until they reach the top if desired...or just left to grow naturally. In late August or early September — about six weeks before killing frost — pinch off top of vine, growing tips of branches and late blossoms to concentrate vigor on fruit development (do this also for melons, cucumbers, squash and pumpkins — pinch off fuzzy ends).

Left: Single Yellow Pear "caged" plant grew to 9' and produced over 2,000 fruits for nibbling and preserves. Several main stems grew over top of ring [see arrow] and then were trained over one side.

- MULCHING. Do not mulch inside of ring until blossoms or first fruit forms. Thereafter, mulch heavily with straw or hay within ring and between rings.

- SUBSEQUENT FEEDING. Excellent results can be obtained by simply watering regularly throughout the growing season with a manure/fish emulsion/water mix (see "Manure tea"). If a further boost is desired once fruit sets, use one of the  special tomato fertilizers low in nitrogen but high in both phosphorus and potash. High nitrogen fertilizers promote excessive foliage growth. Potash generates better fruit development; phosphorus helps plant stand cold weather better. Recommended by a garden center owner are: Science "Tomato Gro" (10-52-17), Ferti-Lome Tomato Food (4-13-7) and Orthos liquid tomato fertilizer (6-18-6). If you use a special tomato "soil" (see "Damping-off a problem?") when you plant the tomatoes, further fertilization may not be necessary.

- VARIATION on the "one-tomato-per-ring" system is a growing method called the "Japanese Ring," "Chinese Ring" or "Compost Ring." Make a ring about the same size or slightly larger, but of chicken wire. Fill the ring in layers with well-rotted manure, compost, grass clippings, bone meal, etc. — just as you would a compost heap, which it is. Set 4-6 tomato plants in a circle *outside* the ring and as they grow, train them up the side by tying them to the chicken wire. Sucker and tie tomato plants in the traditional manner. As the compost cone decomposes, keep adding ingredients and keep it moist. Tomato roots, which spread 2-3', are nourished *continuously* by the rich compost and extraordinary yields have been reported. *You can adapt this same idea if your existing compost pile is of wire or something to which tomatoes can be tied...is not above ground...and is in full sun.*

X-TRA POTENT SOIL FOR TRANSPLANTS gives 'em a strong head start. Try this formula: 1 part sterilized garden soil, 1 part organic peat, 1/3 part tomato "soil," 1/3 part sterilized, screened compost and 1/3 part vermiculite. *To sterilize garden soil or compost,* pour boiling water *slowly* through the mix (about a gallon for standard-size flat) or bake in an oven. To avoid the mess — and much of the odor — of baking soil or compost in an open pan, use a turkey-size oven roasting bag. Bake at 180° for 30 minutes (2-3 hours of baking time no longer is felt to be necessary). Allow the sterilized soil to rest for 24 hours before using. Store leftovers in closed plastic bags.

ANKING ROOT CROPS such as carrots and parsnips by the stalks will leave you with a fistful of tops unless you harvest after a rain or deep watering. If you can't wait, a dandelion weeder does a dandy digging job.

YELLOW PLASTIC DISHPAN — the brighter the better — makes an effective trap for aphids, who for some reason known only to themselves are attracted to anything yellow (see "Red and orange colors"). Fill dishpan 3/4 with water and set in the middle of the garden. Aphids by the droves land on the water and can't get out. They sink to the bottom in a day or two.

YESTERDAY'S NEWSPAPER: (1) use as frost protection — early spring *and* fall; (2) shred some for the compost heap; (3) use as mulch (3-6 layers) — cover with soil or organic mulches for better appearance and to speed decomposition (research has shown there's no danger of black printing ink "leaching" into soil, but there is evidence of minor negative reaction from color inks); (4) use as cutworm collar (see "Cutworms"). Here's the method used by a MGCA member in Minneapolis: "Tear 2" wide strips of newspaper from a complete section (10-20 pages) the full length of the page. Then tear these again in about 4" lengths. After transplanting and watering seedlings, a single strip 2" by 4" is wrapped snugly around each plant stem and the soil pushed in around the plant, filling in the watering depression and covering half-way up the newspaper collar. The whole operation takes very little extra time, since one goes through all the motions of watering and firming the soil around the plant anyway. As the plant stem grows and expands, the newspaper collar expands and eventually sloughs off. Tomatoes, peppers, eggplant, cauliflower, cabbage, broccoli, cucumbers, melons and other crops can be protected in this manner."

ANY TRICK NUMBER 1: While cucumbers are small, put one of the fruits inside any glass bottle with narrow mouth and let it grow inside to giant size. Once it has filled the bottle, cut it off the vine, pour vinegar in and seal. A real eye-popper for the neighborhood children or the bridge club.

ZANY TRICK NUMBER 2 (Memorial Day Special): If you grow white peonies, cut an 8-9" stem, place in *warm* water with red or blue food coloring added. Bloom will absorb color — the longer it soaks, the more intense the color. You also can split a stem in half — put one half in red food coloring, the other half in blue food coloring. Result: red, white and blue flowers.

ZANY TRICK NUMBER 3: When the neighbors aren't around, try talking to your tomatoes, chatting with your cucumbers, praising your peas. While so occupied, scientists tell us you're giving a plant-stimulating boost of extra carbon dioxide. *A much more important benefit, however, is that you're more apt to notice a ready-to-be-harvested vegetable you missed on regular rounds...an overlooked weed...a nibbling hornworm...an early sign of water stress, nutrient deficiency or fungus disease.* Unless certain disease controls are applied at the "just right" time, the *entire* crop can be lost.

ZERO WEATHER can be prime growing weather — if you have indoor lights, particularly the new fluorescents that duplicate the sun exactly and make it easy to grow tomatoes indoors. Be sure to try Burpee's indoor-outdoor tomato Pixie, a hybrid producing plum-size fruit with a "big tomato" flavor. Grown in 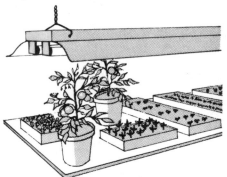 deep containers, the 14-18" vines will produce fruit *all winter* in good sunlight or under lights. Shake branches slightly or place electric toothbrush against stems to aid in pollination or "spot pollinate" blossoms using a watercolor brush or a cotton swab. *Don't wait until fall to buy your Pixie seeds — get 'em in the spring.* Write Burpee for free leaflet on growing Pixie indoors. See photo, page 72.

ZEST FOR VEGETABLE GARDENING? "A to Z Hints for the Vegetable Gardener" represents *just a small sample* of the kind of practical tips on all phases of gardening members receive at every local meeting of the Men's Garden Clubs of America — over 10,000 strong and growing faster than any gourd. (No cultivation hints are necessary for gourds — just plant a seed and run for your life!)

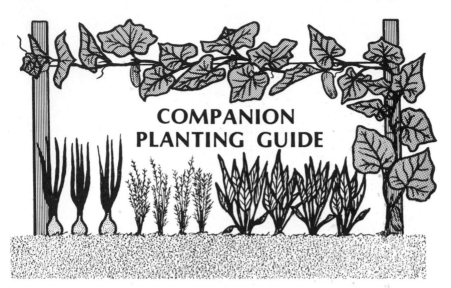

COMPANION PLANTING GUIDE

FRUIT/VEGETABLE	FRIENDS	ENEMIES
Asparagus	Tomatoes, nasturtiums, parsley, basil	Onions, garlic, gladiolus
Beans	Potatoes, beets (bush beans only), carrots, peas, cauliflower, cabbage (bush), eggplant, cucumbers, corn, radishes (pole), summer savory, celery (bush), strawberries, rosemary, petunia, parsnips (bush), sunflower (bush)	Beets and cabbage family (pole beans only), onion family (both), kohlrabi, sunflower (pole), gladiolus, fennel
Beets	Bush beans, cabbage, lettuce, onions, kohlrabi, lima beans	Pole beans
Broccoli	Onion family, herbs. See ''Cabbage.''	See ''Cabbage.''
Brussels Sprouts	Carrots, herbs	See ''Cabbage.''
Cabbage	Beets, carrots, beans (bush), lettuce, spinach, onions, cucumbers, kale, potatoes, celery, herbs (aromatic), dill, sage (repels cabbage butterflies), rosemary, mint*, camomile, nasturtiums	Strawberries, tomatoes, pole beans

NOTE: For additional information about companion planting, see "Secrets of Companion Planting for Successful Gardening" by Louise Riotte [Garden Way Publishing, Charlotte, Vermont 05445] and "Companion Plants and How to Use Them" by Helen Philbrick and Richard Gregg [Devin-Adair Company, One Park Avenue, Old Greenwich, Ct. 06870].

FRUIT/VEGETABLE	FRIENDS	ENEMIES
Cantaloupes	Corn	None
Carrots	Beans, peas, tomatoes, onions, leeks, Brussels sprouts, peppers, cabbage, leaf lettuce, red radishes, chives, rosemary, sage	Dill, celery, parsnips
Cauliflower	See "Cabbage."	See "Cabbage."
Celery	Cabbage, cauliflower, leeks, tomatoes, bush beans, peas	Carrots, parsnips
Corn	Beans, peas, early potatoes, cucumbers, cantaloupes, squash, cabbage, parsley, pumpkin	None
Cucumbers	Beans, peas, corn, tomatoes, cabbage, lettuce, radishes, sunflowers, dill, nasturtiums	Potatoes, aromatic herbs, sage
Eggplant	Beans, peppers	None
Kale	Cabbage, herbs (aromatic)	None
Kohlrabi	Beets, lettuce, onions	Tomatoes, pole beans
Leeks	Celery, carrots, celeriac, onions	Peas, beans
Lettuce	Beets, carrots, radishes (leaf), kohlrabi, strawberries, cabbage, onion family (aids lettuce), basil, cucumbers	None
Lima Beans	Beets, radishes	None
Melons	Corn (cantaloupe)	None
Onion Family (including garlic)	Beets, tomatoes, broccoli, peppers, kohlrabi, lettuce, cabbage, leeks, summer savory, carrots, strawberries, camomile, parsnips, turnips	Beans, peas, asparagus

90

FRUIT/VEGETABLE	FRIENDS	ENEMIES
Parsley	Asparagus, tomatoes, corn	None
Parsnips	Bush beans, peppers, potatoes, peas, radishes, onions, garlic	Carrots, celery, caraway
Peas	Radishes, carrots, cucumbers, corn, beans, turnips, celery, potatoes	Onion family, gladiolus
Peppers	Tomatoes, eggplant, onions, carrot, parsnips	None
Potatoes	Beans, cabbage, corn, peas, marigolds, horseradish (planted at corners), eggplant (as a lure for Colorado potato beetle), parsnips	Pumpkin, squash, cucumbers, turnips, rutabagas, tomatoes, sunflowers, raspberry
Pumpkin	Corn, eggplant, radishes	Potatoes
Radishes	Peas, pole beans, leaf lettuce, nasturtiums, cucumbers, carrots, lima beans, chervil, parsnips	None
Soybeans	Grows with anything, helps everything	None
Spinach	Cabbage, strawberries	None
Squash	Corn, nasturtiums	Potatoes
Strawberries	Lettuce (as a border), spinach, beans, onions, borage	Cabbage
Tomatoes	Asparagus, peppers, celery, onions, carrots, cucumbers, basil, parsley, mint*, chives, marigolds, nasturtiums	Dill, potatoes, cabbage, kohlrabi, fennel
Turnips and Rutabagas	Peas and most vegetables, including onion family	Potatoes

* Mint is handy to have around — but it's a notorious spreader. To contain roots, grow it in a large flower pot sunk to ground level. Locate under an outdoor faucet if you can, as mint will welcome the occasional drippings.

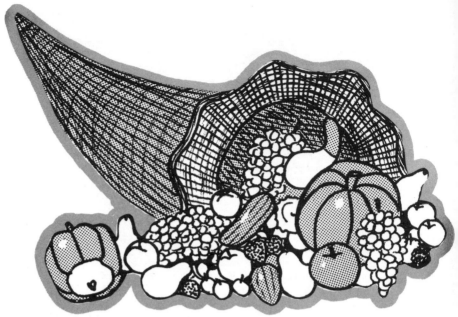

HARVESTING HINTS
AND STORAGE SAVVY . . .
WHAT TO DO AND <u>WHEN</u> TO DO IT !

Knowing the "just right" stage of maturity for home-grown vegetables from Artichokes to Zucchini is an "art" that comes with experience. Check these A to Z guidelines and tips and you'll not only avoid needless waste, but enjoy peak flavor throughout the growing season. Preserving your garden's bounty also requires some practical "know-how" to avoid losses. Pickling, preserving, canning, freezing, drying and the time-honored ways of storage indoors and outdoors are the basic methods of "saving" for later savoring. The first five are covered extensively in readily-available cookbooks, special guides, extension bureau publications, etc. and — in some instances — in this book. Emphasis here will be on both new and traditional methods of storage appropriate for most parts of the country.

STORAGE METHODS. Essentials for successful storage are proper temperature, humidity and ventilation...which vary according to the type of vegetable. Here's a summary of some of the major types of storage facilities or ideas. One or more will fit all crops suitable for storage. The A to Z listing on the following pages refers to the type(s) of storage applicable by numbers 1 through 8:

(1) ROOT CELLAR, a ventilated "cold room" underground — usually with a dirt floor that can be sprinkled occasionally to retain high humidity. One of the finest methods of storage, but — alas — few gardeners have 'em anymore. A popular alternative is...

(2) CELLAR STORAGE. An ideal location for a "storage closet" is a well-ventilated, cool basement with or without central heat. Ideally, storage area should be located in the northeast corner (away from the furnace) and near one or two windows to provide for ventilation. Windows should be shaded to keep out light. Insulating partitions should be added if the furnace is nearby. Construct walls of 2 X 4s and siding material — boards or plywood. Line walls and ceilings with 1/4" wire mesh to keep out rodents. Styrofoam rigid insulation board, aluminum-sheathed Fiberglas, rigid foamglass and urethane boards also can be used for insulating rooms. Dirt floor is ideal; if cement, sprinkle occasionally with water to provide humidity. If you have a sloping cellar door with an outside stairwell leading into the basement, this area can be converted into cold storage space fairly easily and at little expense. Install inside door to keep out basement heat. This area can be expanded inward, too... insulate extra wall space created. Cellar window wells? These take advantage of outdoor cold and indoor heat and can be used for storing small quantities of vegetables by covering the well with boards. Add some kind of insulation (even straw or hay) on top of boards, then place a waterproof cover across the window well. Hardware cloth "lining" will keep out rodents.

(3) IN GROUND STORAGE. With a protective topping of mulch (straw, hay, grass clippings, etc.), parsnips, salsify and — in many areas — carrots and turnips can be left in the ground over winter.

(4) HAY BALE STORAGE (Top of Ground). Build a rectangle of hay bales; center should be partially filled with hay, with vegetables on top. For a "lid," add more bales of hay. For ventilation, place a rock under one or more top bales; remove rocks during freezing weather. Inside storage area can be lined with 1/4" wire mesh if rodents are a problem. Suitable for most root crops.

(5) MOUND STORAGE (Top of Ground). Place straw or hay on the ground; place vegetables on top. Mound with additional mulch, then soil. Place boards over soil arranged in "teepee" fashion; top with tar paper circle large enough to cover vegetables. A covered

vent can be inserted at the top to extend through soil to straw or hay layer (cap vent during freezing weather). Dig drainage ditch around the mound.

(6) TILE STORAGE PIT. Large tiles (18" x 30" or 24" x 24") can be used to line pits located in an area with excellent drainage and shaded from the sun. At bottom of pit, throw in several shovelfuls of gravel and add a couple of bricks. On top of bricks, place boxes, baskets, etc. of such vegetables as potatoes, beets and carrots. A wood box with hardware cloth screen attached to open end (for rodent protection) should be placed above tiles (screen side down). Insulation, plus a waterproof material, should be placed in and around the box. Weigh down "topping" with a brick or two. Alternative: bury a 20-gallon garbage can in the ground; vegetables can be placed directly into the can.

(7) BARREL PIT. Partially bury a carefully cleaned, well-made barrel set horizontally with top slanted upward and above ground and covered with a board. Portion of barrel under ground should be about 8-12" deep. Add a few stones underneath for drainage. Mound about 18-20" of soil around bottom and sides; insulate with 3' straw or hay; cover with two wide boards positioned in inverted "V" shape to hold straw or hay and shed rain. In areas of severe cold, barrel can be buried somewhat deeper than indicated above. This storage method also may be used for fruit.

(8) SOIL-PIT STORAGE (can be used in winter areas with deep soil temperature of about 52°). Ideal location is on sloping ground for drainage. Neatly cut out pit area about 3' wide, 6' long and 2' deep. Construct storage box to fit hole. Use 2 X 4s for frame, sides are 1/4" hardware cloth carefully kept tight to keep out rodents. Bottom is wood as is the top, which is hinged. Place layer of washed builder's sand on the bottom of the pit; then place a neat layer of vegetables (carrots, beets, parsnips, potatoes, turnips, etc.). Cover first layer of vegetables with sand, repeat layering until pit is filled. Keep a record as to where different vegetables are located; or mix vegetables of each kind in each layer. Cover pit with four bales of straw or hay; topped with tarpaulin or plastic sheet to keep off snow. This storage method has provided good-quality vegetables as late as May and early June. Also may be used for cabbage, celery and other crops.

Mound Storage

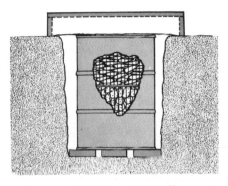

Storage Pit Using 20-Gallon Can (see "Tile Storage Pit")

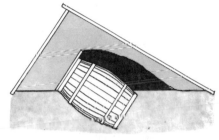

Barrel Pit

TIPS TO REMEMBER WHEN HARVESTING CROPS FOR STORAGE:

- Vegetables to be stored should be left in the garden as long as possible without danger of freezing.

- Only sound, top-quality produce should be stored. Because of the fast spread of decay organisms, any injured vegetables should be set aside and used first.

- Handle crops reserved for storage carefully to avoid bruising or the slightest scratch or scrape. Squash and pumpkins, for example, should be handled "like eggs."

- Mature, hard-ripe vegetables store the longest. Green garden crops should *not* be stored. (Green tomatoes are an exception.)

- Right size and maturity for storage comes mostly from *summer sowing*. Large beets, carrots, etc. sown in the spring are too large and woody for top quality storage; these should be used in mid-summer for table use and canning.

- ROOT CROPS. Digging fork is best to avoid injury to roots. Always cut off tops of root crops — but not closer than 1/2" to crown — as soon as removed from soil. Considerable moisture is lost from roots through leaves if leaves are left on and this causes shriveling of the roots.

- Vegetables for storage should not be washed. Use a *soft* brush to remove any soil clinging to roots. All should be stored with a dry surface (celery and similar crops should have moisture around the roots, *but the foliage must be dry to avoid rot*).

- Shriveling in vegetables needing moist conditions (beets, carrots, parsnips) can be prevented by sprinkling walls and floors with water as needed during the winter. Pans of water also may be set out in storage area.

- Wooden apple boxes, if used indoors for storage, should be stacked with furring strips between units and the floor to permit full air circulation. Orange crates, mesh bags and discarded nylon hoses are excellent for onion storage.

- Fruits should never be stored with potatoes, turnips or cabbage. Gases released from apples in respiration can sprout potatoes; cabbage and turnips transmit their odors to pears and apples.

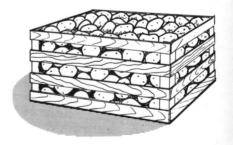

A TO Z GUIDE

Harvesting Hints

Storage Savvy

HARVESTING HINTS FROM ARTICHOKES TO ZUCCHINI

STORAGE SAVVY - HOW TO SAVE FOR LATER SAVORING

Artichoke (Globe)

Cut unripened flower heads before bracts begin to separate. Cut with 1-1/2" of stem; flower should be about the size of an orange.

Use fresh, freeze, etc. Buds not harvested ripen into huge, violet pink thistle blossoms and these can be dried for flower arrangements (will last several years).

Artichoke (Jerusalem)

Freezing improves flavor for this vegetable form of sunflower. Dig tubers as late as possible in the fall (after top growth ceases), during a winter thaw or in early spring (before sprouting begins).

Best taste is right after harvesting, so dig only what you need for one meal.

Once soil has frozen crust, mulch bed with thick layer of leaves. Dig as needed. Can be stored in airtight container in refrigerator or layered in moist sand or sawdust in a cool place.

Use any of the storage methods previously described.

Asparagus

Harvest asparagus just before it is to be cooked. Snapping spears off at the surface rather than cutting below the surface increases yields. Keep picked or spears will shoot up into ferns and end the harvest. Spears should be from 6-8″ above ground (unless heads begin to bud out). Spears taller than 8″ have passed best harvest stage. (See "Asparagus hints.")

Beans

Snap or string beans. Pick regularly or production will stop. Pull pods off carefully while holding stems with free hand (rough picking can break off stems and destroy plants). Harvest in morning, after dew has disappeared from the foliage. Pods should be bright in color, thick and fleshy; seeds should not yet have begun to swell. Best when 3-6″ long. Pole beans to be served as snap beans should be picked before they swell. When pods become round, shell and serve fresh.

Wax beans should be buttery yellow.

Lima beans. Limas are excellent when the seeds are used green. Harvest when pods first start to bulge with the enlarged seed. Pods must still be green and not have turned yellowish. Mature beans may be dried.

Use fresh, freeze, etc.

Matured dry beans of all kinds and varieties are ready to harvest when a majority of the pods are dry and papery. Shell beans reserved for storage on a dry day. To dry, spread on screens in airy place such as garage or attic (if well ventilated). Beans should dry in about three weeks depending on the weather.

Here are three ways to beat the bean weevil:

(1) Store beans in cans in an unheated garage or porch (beans won't freeze). Temperature of storage area isn't important, but it *must be dry;*

(2) Dip beans in boiling water for one minute and spread them out to dry;

(3) Or heat beans (spread thinly) in an oven for one hour at 135°

"Southern peas" and "Soybeans" — see separate listings.

Store in jars, tin containers or boxes or — if a large quantity — in tight cotton (not burlap) bags.

Beets

For tops, harvest when roots are 1-1 1/2 " across. For roots, 2-3" in diameter is about right. Once they reach 3" in diameter, don't leave in ground more than 10 days or quality deteriorates. Second sowing in early July gives crop for fall use and winter storage. Harvest after 30° nights.

No curing is required. When hard frosts are expected, dig when soil is dry. Cut off tops about 1" above crown to prevent "bleeding." Cool temperature (never above 40°) is recommended, with sufficient humidity — up to 95% — to prevent shriveling. Beets may be packed in bins, boxes or cans, surrounded by straw, or layered in slightly moist sand, or placed in an outdoor storage pit. Storage methods 1, 2, 4, 5, 6, 7 and 8 may be used.

Some gardeners have brought beets through the winter by mulching heavily, but only a few should be tried this way.

Broccoli

Harvest when flower cluster is in the tight bud stage, leaving about 6-8" of stem (see "Broccoli hints"). Some say broccoli cut in the morning has better flavor; others prefer to cut just before cooking. Harvest lateral flower clusters in the same manner. If clusters flower, cut immediately and discard.

Use fresh or freeze.

Brussels sprouts

Cut off lower leaves when sprouts first open. Lowest sprouts should be picked first and before the lower leaves turn yellow. Twist off green sprouts

Light frost improves flavor. May be left in ground until very cold weather; moderate freezing will not injure sprouts. Where winters are severe, harvest can be

Brussels sprouts [continued]

when they are 1-1 1/2" across or about the size of a shelled walnut and cook at once. Breaking off lower leaves and stem where each sprout is forming hastens the crop. Top sprouts will get larger if growing tip of plant is pinched off when lower sprouts begin to grow well.

Cabbage (including Chinese Cabbage)

Harvest cabbage when heads feel hard and solid by cutting head off at base with sharp knife (see "Cabbage hints").

***

Chinese cabbage should be harvested when "heads" are firm and compact; cut off at ground level. Chinese cabbage is frost resistant, so it should be left in the garden as long as possible to become mature. Store like celery.

***

Coleslaw and cooked cabbage freeze well. To eliminate cooking odors with cabbage (also broccoli and Brussels sprouts), place a heel of bread on top of vegetable, replace lid.

prolonged by: (1) taking up plants with a spade (leave soil on roots); (2) snapping off roots; (3) laying plants on bed of leaves or straw with extra soil packed around roots; and (4) covering with 6-12" of leaves or straw for added insulation. Entire plant also can be pulled up and stored in cool cellar or pit — or trench like celery (which see). Also see storage methods 1, 2, 3, 5, 6, 7 and 8. Freezes well.

Do not allow heads to freeze. Reserve the *heaviest* heads for storage (not necessarily the largest). Pull up cabbage by roots (when weather has turned cold) and hang upside down in a cool place such as an unheated garage for 7-10 days. Then cut away the roots and stems and loose outer leaves. Wrap heads in several layers of newspapers (or burlap), pack loosely into barrel, boxes or bins and store in a cold, damp area. Because of the strong odor, cabbage is frequently stored outdoors in one of the storage arrangements using damp sand or soil. Stems and roots then can be left on. In moderate climates, cabbage can be stored layered in hay right in the garden (with roots and stem). To shed rain, cover with a plastic sheet.

Cantaloupes — See "Melons..."

Carrots

When carrots are mature, orange crown will appear at soil line. Dig, never pull up by stalks (see "Carrot hints"). Carrots can stay in ground with mulch for protection until just before a hard frost and in some areas over the winter (cover with about a foot of leaves or straw before the ground has frozen to make digging easier; add a waterproof cover). Or carrots can be dug in early autumn and stored. *Whenever* carrots are dug, always clip fern tops immediately — leaving about 2". When pulled for storage, carrots should be allowed to dry in the open air for a half-day.

Worst way to store carrots is in dry sand. Try packing in sawdust in large tin cans with no cover. Dampen sawdust occasionally during winter. Place a newspaper over top to hold moisture. Crocks also may be used. Success has been reported with cardboard boxes, too. Place layer of newspaper on bottom and pour in about 2" of peat moss. Repeat layers, dampening each layer of peat. In general, carrots require moist conditions and an area with low temperatures — never above 40°. Carrots and other root crops can be stored in a dry room if water is added, as needed, directly to the vegetable or by storing in closed containers (large crocks, metal cans, barrels, tight wooden boxes, etc.). If a root cellar is available, carrots need only be placed in bags. See storage methods 1, 2, 3, 4, 5, 6, 7 and 8.

Cauliflower

Harvest edible curds when still compact, before they open and become ricey. If the flowers break and spread, quality is lost...so watch cauliflower *closely.* Ripened heads left on plant rot very quickly. Head should be ready 2-3 weeks after head has been blanched. Cut head with a sharp knife where it meets main stem.

Unlike cabbage, cauliflower will not withstand chilly weather.

Will keep for several weeks if whole plant is pulled up and hung upside down in a cool, dark place such as a basement.

See storage methods 1 and 2. Freezes well.

Celeriac

May be harvested early when roots are only 2" around; roots are 4" across when mature. Pull up by the tops, clean off side roots, twist off tops.

Store in a cool place layered in moist sand.

Storage methods 1 and 2 are ideal.

Celery

A few stalks can be harvested early, as soon as sufficient growth has taken place. Once a tight head has formed, cut plants at base (just beneath crown). Celery also may be cut about 2" below ground. Trim away outer stalks. Will withstand light frosts if hilled.
Special growing tip: Some gardeners report that celery grows better if grown in a *tight circle* (about 2' in diameter) rather than in a row. Water from inside of circle.

Lift roots with a fork, leaving a considerable lump of soil attached to roots. Leave tops dry; don't wash. Place upright in a 2' deep trench (closely packed). Covered with a 2' mulch, "trenched" celery will keep well into freezing weather. Roots also may be placed in slightly moist sand or soil and stored in a cold basement (ideally 32° - 34°). Keep away from cabbage or turnips to avoid odor contamination. See storage methods 1, 2, 6, 7 and 8.

Collards

Let first six to eight leaves develop to full size to sustain plant before starting to pick. For continuous growth, never harvest central growing point. Clip off and cook young, tender leaves (including the stem) when about the size of your hand.

Flavor is improved by frost.

Mature plants are frost hardy, similar to kale.

Protect with straw or hay mulch as coldest weather arrives.

Corn

Silks begin to turn dark brown when ready. Feel the ear. If the husk seems to be firm and not yield much, chances are the ear

Best not stored — but cooked immediately after picking. If corn must be held for a short time, husk and refrigerate im-

Corn [continued]

is mature. Check further by pulling down tip of ear and checking the kernels. They should be nicely filled out, and will "squirt" a milky juice when dented with the fingernail. (See "Corn hints.")

Cucumber

Pick when cucumbers are deep green, before they turn yellow. With most types, harvest at 2-3" for sweet pickles, 5-6" for dills and 6-8" for slicing. Most important harvesting rule: keep vines picked — up to 4 or 5 times a week during peak of production — to encourage continuous production. When picking, roll brittle vines over gently and hold firmly while picking; roll back into place (never lift vines high above the ground). Don't harvest when plants are wet and forget about weeds once vines are mature (pulling weeds disturbs cucumber roots and can cause wilting). (See "Cucumber hints.")

Eggplant

Snip off fruit with kitchen shears or use sharp knife (never twist off). Best when fruits are 4-5" in diameter (about 2/3 grown) and a glossy purple black. Fruit is too old when skin starts to dull. Allow short stem to remain on each fruit. (See "Eggplant hints.")

mediately in plastic bags. If freezing, reserve smaller ears for freezing on the cob; cut kernels from larger ears (see "Freezing tips for corn-on-the-cob"). Late corn maturing in the fall will be sweetest for freezing.

Cucumbers can be stored a week or two at 45° - 50° in a dark place.

Cucumber Bush Whopper, a 1977 introduction and a Park Seed exclusive. This compact cucumber produces fruit 6-8" long. A dwarf, mound-shaped plant with no runners, it makes an excellent plant for small gardens or pot culture.

In cooler areas, protect with plastic canopy toward end of season (see "Frost damage"). Before killing frost, pick all fruits, store indoors in a cool, dark place. Or pull up entire plant and hang by roots. Eggplant does not store well for longer than a week or two.

103

HARVESTING HINTS

Endive

Outer leaves on this lettuce substitute may be used without harvesting the plant. Or entire plant can be used for salads. Flavor improves with cool weather. For milder flavor, gather outer leaves and tie loosely. Hearts thus blanched are mild and tender.

Lift with a fork and leave soil attached to roots. Place upright, packed together- er closely and tightly in a trench, outdoor pit or cold basement.

Garlic

Garlic is ready when the tops have died down, as with onions.

Cure in open air and mottled sunlight for two days. Clip off leaves with shears and store bulbs in open trays in an airy, outdoor building to cure until husks are paper dry or braid the stems and hang clusters until completely dried. Store cured bulbs in a cool, dry room and they'll keep well all winter. Don't allow to freeze or they'll rot. Also see "Onions."

Gourds

Don't harvest too early, only when frost threatens. Stem should be very hard. Leave 2" of stem attached on smaller gourds. On larger gourds, leave up to 7" of stem; hang with wire to dry. Small gourds take at least several months to dry; large gourds often need the entire winter. Seeds rattle when ready.

Keep gourds in a warm, dry place until thoroughly dried. Mold will form, but this is expected (see "Gourds"). In the spring, wash in warm, soapy water; scrape with knife and rub with steel wool to remove light film. Wipe with a soft towel, then set aside to become *absolutely dry* before applying shellac.

Herbs

Use fresh or dry. Cut early in morning, after foliage has dried. Herbs grown for their leaves and intended for drying and storage should be harvested just as the flower buds start to open and after first flower has unfolded.

Drying for storage in glass jars or other airtight containers: Strip leaves from stem, remove flower heads. Place leaves loosely and thinly on mesh-bottomed trays or on window screen so air can circulate. Dry in warm, dry room. No direct sunlight should reach herbs being dried. Stir leaves each morning for 4-5 days or until completely dry. Herbs also can be hung in small bundles to dry. Or they can be spread out on a cookie sheet and placed in oven for 2-3 hours at *lowest* heat setting. Leave oven door slightly ajar (but without light on).

Horseradish

Dig roots in early fall, trim rootlets, wash and dry.

In most areas, can be left in the ground over winter and dug as needed. Also may be layered in damp sand in a cool, dry place.

Kale

Twist off outer leaves as needed. Leaves should be bright green and crisp with firm texture. Dark green "heavy" leaves are overmature, tough and bitter. Kale also may be harvested by using the entire plant.

No need to store — just let it keep growing right into winter.

Kohlrabi

Thickened base of stem should be no larger than 2-3 inches. Cut off plant just below the "bulb" and dispose of rest of

Quality is improved by touch of frost. Kale will furnish greens in winter if mulched with about a foot of loose straw or hay.

Kohlrabi [continued]

plant. Young kohlrabi is excellent eaten raw or steamed without peeling. More mature kohlrabi should be peeled, sliced or diced and boiled in a very little salted water.

Can be stored — after removal of leaves and roots — at about 32° - 34° in a place with 95% humidity (such as root cellar or basement "cellar storage").

Leeks

Use thinnings as scallions. Pull when fully mature — roughly an inch in diameter. Sow seeds in late spring or early summer for use in winter.

In milder climates, may be left in ground over winter. In severe cold areas, dig before hard frosts and layer in moist sand in a cool place.

Lettuce

Leaf lettuce: cut only as much as you can use at one time, using scissors or a knife. Cut entire plant off 1" above base rather than taking off one leaf at a time. Add fertilizer boost. Plants will grow back and the new growth will be the best. *Head, Bibb and Cos:* cut off at base in the same manner. See "Lettuce hints."

Pick late crop when dry.

Refrigerate to maintain crispness. Lettuce can be stored for several weeks in a very cold root cellar. May be grown inside during the winter under lights or in a cold frame.

Melons and muskmelons

Cut — don't pull — watermelons from the vine. Leave a short stem always. Check *all* melons in the morning for ripeness, before melons get warm.

Watermelon: Ripe watermelons have a dull thudding sound rather than a sharp sound when thumped (see "Punk"). Other ripeness indicators: brown

Only fresh, well-ripened fruit should be frozen. Melon balls are ideal use. If further ripening is needed, ripen at room temperature. Cantaloupe will never get sweeter if taken from the vine too green; they will simply soften.

Melons can be stored for a week or two at 40° - 45°.

Melons and muskmelons [continued]

tendrils on stem near fruit; yellowish rather than white color where melon touches ground; rough, slightly ridged feel to surface.

Muskmelon [cantaloupe]. Should be picked when netting on skin becomes rounded and flesh between netting turns from green to tan color. Don't test skin with fingernail — rot may set in. Press lightly on stem with thumb at the point the stem joins the fruit. If stem parts with a slight pull, it's ready.

Honeydew and casaba. When ripe, these have a sweet odor and a creamy-yellow surface color.

Persian. Smell blossom ends. If smell is sweet and fruity, fruits probably are ripe.

Burpee's Ambrosia Hybrid Cantaloupe

Mustard greens

Snap off only leaves (don't pull plants); growing tip will produce new leaves. Leaves should be picked just before they mature. Plants should be kept cut back to hold off flowering. Leaves become tough and bitter after flowering.

Use immediately as cooked greens or in salads. Also may be frozen.

Like lettuce, fast-growing mustard greens are easy to grow inside under lights or in a sunny window.

Okra

Pods should be harvested when young and tender — about 2-3" long and never over 4". Tough-

Fresh picked okra freezes well, Cut off stem, but don't cut into the seed pod or sticky juices

Okra [continued]

ness test: if you can't cut the stem easily with a knife, okra will be too tough to eat. Keep mature pods picked off to maintain vigor in plants. Pick at least every other day during peak growing season.

Onions

Pinch off all seed pods as they form on the tops of the stalks.

Once about 75% of onion tops have begun to dry and fall, bend over remaining tops lightly with a rake to divert growing energy to the bulb (don't bruise neck, as this will shorten storage life). When all the tops are completely withered and turned brown, dig onions and cut the stem, leaving 2-3" attached. Place in mottled sun for several days to initially dry out and toughen the skin. An additional drying period of 2-4 weeks in a protected place such as an open shed is not too much to draw the excess water from the bulb. Don't remove soil until thoroughly cured; dirt then will come off without washing. Use thick-necked onions first, as they won't keep. Note regarding storage: American onions store best; Bermuda onions are not good keepers. Onions grown from seed often have the best storage qualities.

(See "Onion hints.")

will flow out. Pods may be stored for several days in a cool room. Sprinkle frequently with water to maintain high humidity. Be sure there's good air circulation in storage room and store in *open* container.

When onions are mature, don't "store" in soil or bulbs will rot.

Only firm onions should be stored. Once cured, place in slatted crates or course mesh bags and store in a cold, dry, dark place (floor of a closet is good, as is an attic). Onions will stand freezing, but should not be handled while frozen as this will spoil them. Some gardeners don't cut the stems and "French" braid onions using baler twine.

Storage area selected should have a temperature ranging from 33° - 45° and about 60%-75% humidity.

Parsley

Pick in early morning, before delicate oils have evaporated. Pinch off older outer stems.

Use fresh or dry as described under "Herbs." Grow inside during the winter as a houseplant.

Parsnips

Dig (never pull up by tops) parsnips as needed from late summer through fall. In warm climates, dig as soon as roots are mature. In cold climates, cover row with organic mulch or newspapers when a hard frost is predicted. Flavor of roots is improved by frost and freezing. When harvesting, always cut off tops immediately. (See "Parsnip hints.")

Parsnips may be left in the ground over winter in many areas for harvest as needed and before new growth starts. Simply cut off tops and toss on about a foot of loose mulch like straw. Once freezing weather arrives, roots also may be dug for storage. Leave roots in the open for at least several hours to dry. Store in soil in a cold basement, garage or outdoor pit.

Peas

Check peas closely — every day when pods of good size start appearing. As with corn, pick immediately before using as sweetness is quickly dissipated — especially if temperature is high. Pick smooth-seeded varieties when pods are well filled out and before seeds become hard and wrinkled. They should be a bright green color; they're too old when pods lose brightness and turn light or yellowish green. Sweeter varieties and edible-podded peas are picked when young, just as soon as seeds have begun to form, and when they're succulent and free of fiber. If edible-podded peas are left on the vine until peas fully form, these can be shelled and eaten like other peas.

To extend the harvest, plant early, midseason and late varieties (see "Pea hints").

Peas will keep for several days in the refrigerator, but ideally should be eaten or frozen immediately after picking (see "Peas in a pillowcase").

Peppers

Cut firm, crisp peppers with a sharp knife, leaving a 1/2" stem. Harvest only mature or near-mature peppers (small ones aren't very good). Peppers may be picked when skin is green or when it turns red. Gather large peppers regularly to keep plant producing. Peppers can often be protected during light frosts by covering plants with a clear plastic canopy. (See "Pepper hints" and "Frost damage.")

Hot peppers: allow to fully vine ripen, then hang to dry.

Potatoes

Early varieties are ready when flowers form. For later varieties, yellowing and dying of vines indicate tubers are full size. Probe carefully with a spading fork. As "new" potatoes reach a desirable size, they may be harvested if done carefully to avoid damaging the plant. Never dig potatoes for storage while the tops are green; they won't keep well. Best time to harvest late potatoes is several weeks after a killing frost (but never allow tubers to freeze in the ground). (See "Potatoes.")

To determine best storage potatoes, rub skins. If a skin rubs off easily, that potato is still green and should be set aside for kitchen use.

When killing frost threatens, pull up entire plant and hang in a cool place to allow peppers to ripen. Mature peppers will keep for several weeks in the refrigerator crisper, or in a dark place at least 40° - 45°.

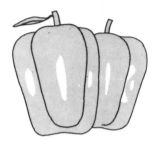

The day you dig potatoes for storage should be above 45° and the soil should not be wet. Keep protected from sun and wind and handle carefully to avoid bruising. Brush off dirt. Place outside in the shade to dry off and set the skins. Cure potatoes 10-14 days at 80° - 85° to decrease losses in storage. Place in a slated crate or basket; store in a dark, humid place. Cover with bags or newspapers to keep out light. At about 50°, potatoes will remain in good condition several months. For longer storage, hold at 50° for two weeks after digging, then store at 34° - 41° to prevent sprouting. If sprouting occurs in early spring, sprinkle lightly with table salt. Never store potatoes with apples.

Pumpkins

Slip a board underneath ripening pumpkins to keep them from turning white or rotting where they touch the ground. Once orange skin color darkens, the skin becomes tough and vines dry up, they're ready — but must be protected from hard frosts if left in the garden. Pumpkin leaves usually give ample protection during light frosts, but a couple of handfuls of straw is a good safeguard. When harvesting for storage, cut (don't pull) pumpkins from the vines and leave a 3-4" stem or they won't store well. Handle fruit very carefully to avoid bruises or scratches. Don't wash fruits before storing.

Radishes

Harvest summer radishes regularly, when shoulders first appear through the soil. Left in the ground, ripe radishes get tough and woody (and, in warm weather, often wormy). If you keep radishes well watered in the summer, they won't be "hot."

Rhubarb

Once rhubarb is in the third year, harvest in early spring when the plant has grown a full stand of stalks. Never *cut* stalks — just grasp outside stalks when they reach 12-18" in length and yank, twisting slight-

Must be cured before storing. Just leave in the field after cutting for two weeks. Or cure in a garage or covered shed if rainy weather prevails. If weather is near freezing, cure indoors at about 70° for several days. Once cured, place gently on shelves separated from each other in a dry, airy, warm, dim place at about 50° - 55°. Furnace room, if not too warm, may be used. Examine every few weeks for mold. If mold occurs, wipe fruit carefully with a cloth made slightly oily with vegetable oil.

Above instructions also apply to winter squash.

Winter radishes can stay right in the row until hard frosts. Store layered in moist sand in a cool place (just above freezing is ideal).

Storage methods 1 and 2 are best.

Freezes well. To force in winter: (1) In late fall, dig around roots you intend to force; (2) allow the ball with the roots to freeze solid for a month or so; (3) take root ball into the basement, place in a box of earth and

Rhubarb [continued]

ly. Leave a few stalks on each plant for better production. And, of course, never eat rhubarb leaves.

Rutabagas

Can stand considerable frost. Unlike turnips, tops are inedible. Harvest after frost, but don't let roots freeze.

Salsify ("Oyster Plant")

Roots may be dug when ample size. Never pull up too forcibly or by tops.

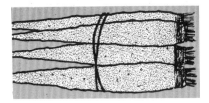

Southern peas
(cowpeas, table peas, field peas)

For fresh peas, pick pods when still green and of the desired size. For drying, pods can remain on plants until they turn a straw yellow or brown color.

water. Keep at about 60° and exclude light. Pink stalks for cooking should be ready in 3-4 weeks.

Well-mulched rutabagas can be stored in the ground and dug as needed; flavor improves after a few frosts. Pull and top, however, before roots are injured by extreme cold. Indoor storage: Dip cleaned roots in melted paraffin, let dry, and store in moist sand in a cold (but not freezing) garage or basement. Rutabagas can be stored undipped in a cool place with good air circulation, such as a vented root cellar.

Like parsnips, salsify may be left in the ground over winter for use in early spring (cover with mulch). Or roots may be dug in the fall (trim tops at least 1" above root) and stored in moist sand in a cool basement or garage or by using any of the storage methods described earlier.

May be canned, frozen or dried.

***

Drying hints: see "Beans" in this section.

HARVESTING HINTS	STORAGE SAVVY

Soybeans

Soybeans to be eaten fresh should be harvested as soon as they plump up in the pods.

For drying, leave on the vine until pods and leaves turn yellow.

Freezes well, or may be dried. To shell easily: soak in boiling water about 5 minutes, then just pop beans out of the end of the pod. Drying hints: see "Beans" in this section.

Spinach

The traditional way to harvest spinach is to nip off outer leaves. Discard stems if stringy. Leave center sprouts to form new leaves.

Cook early pickings, or use in salads with lettuce, chard, etc.

You'll get a lot more spinach, however, harvesting the entire plant instead of taking only the outer leaves. More tender, too. Entire plants may be harvested as soon as they have 4-5 leaves by cutting off at base just below lowest leaf. When three or four new leaves appear, *cut all plants back again.*

Harvest entire crop immediately when flower buds begin to form in the center of the plant.

New Zealand Spinach: once well-established, break leaves from branches 3" from the top. Pick only the side leaves.

(See "Spinach.")

Ideal cooked fresh or used in salads. Also freezes well. Will keep for short time in refrigerator.

New Zealand Spinach: Green leaves tend to be a little bitter when used in salads. Best to boil; change the boiling water once.

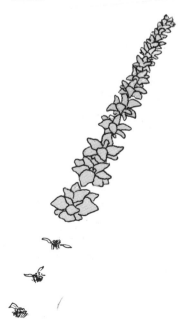

Squash - Summer

Ideally, harvest cylindrical types when 6-8" long (3" across for patty pans) before rind hardens. Depending on variety, skins should be dark, glossy green or yellow. Fruits are usable, even if giant size, as long as your fingernail can easily penetrate the skin. Keep picked for production until frost. Keep checking plants, as zucchini and other summer squash develop quickly. They're usually ready only a few days after blossoming.

Will keep for several weeks in a cool, dark place. If they become soft, discard.

Squash - Winter

Pick only mature, ripe squash.

Acorn squash should have a dark green color, be hard and have an orange or yellow spot where it touches the ground. Butternut squash will have a hard skin and will be a buff or tan color when mature. Buttercup squash will have a very hard rind and be a dark green color with a few small yellow or orange striations in the "cap" when mature.

Leave on vine until stem shrivels. Pick after vines have dried but before frosts. The skins should be hard enough to resist the pressure of your thumbnail. *Leave about a 4" stem on each fruit* (under no circumstances should the fruit be stored without a stem).

Undamaged fruits will keep for months and perhaps even to spring. For storage hints, see "Pumpkins."

HARVESTING HINTS

Sweet potatoes

May be dug when large enough for use — usually when foliage begins to yellow. Harvest full crop as soon as touched by frost. Cut vine tops from roots early in the day to prevent bitter juices from going back into the tubers. Lift roots carefully with a fork to avoid damage (injured sweet potatoes rot easily in storage). Leave a good stem on each sweet potato.

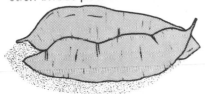

Swiss chard

Plants will produce continuously until killed by frost on a "cut and come again" basis.

Entire plants can be cut off 1" above ground; they'll grow again and again . . . and the new tender growth is the best. If the crop gets ahead of you — or if you want just a little for salads — harvest the outer leaves, giving leaves a sharp twist.

Break off leaves about an inch above the ground.

Tomatoes

Harvest at ripeness stage most appealing to you — up to dead ripe. Keep picked for better production, but don't pick when

STORAGE SAVVY

Cure well before storage, and don't wash. Hold potatoes in a well-ventilated place where temperatures are fairly high (80° - 85°) for about 10-21 days. Humidity also should be high — about 90%. This special curing period is necessary to eliminate excess water, convert some starch to sugar and cause "corking over" of any cuts in the skin. After curing, store in a well-ventilated place at a temperature of about 50° - 60°, with moderate humidity. Consider the furnace room. Don't handle or move potatoes during storage until time for use.

Use fresh in salads or cook like spinach — mixing large and small leaves together. Save some for Swiss Chard Pie (which see). Also freezes well.

When killing frost is on its way, harvest all remaining fruits on the vines except those just beginning to form. *Important:*

Tomatoes [continued]

plants are wet. To protect during early frosts, cover plants with newspapers, sheets, clear plastic canopies, etc. (see "Frost damage"). Harvest remaining crop when killing frost threatens. Entire plant may be pulled and hung by roots in a cool, dark place for slow ripening or individual fruits may be picked.

***

Mature green tomatoes can be stored at 65° - 70°; ripe tomatoes should be held at 50°.

Ripe tomatoes can be kept in the refrigerator for about two weeks. Ripe tomatoes also may be *frozen whole* for use in soups, roasts and stews. Wipe off each fruit with damp paper towel, wipe dry and just place in the freezer (or put in plastic

don't just snap off tomatoes, but cut off the vine carefully leaving a 2" stem on each fruit.

Near ripe, as well as green tomatoes, will retain "vine ripened" flavor only if they're picked with stem attached.

Cover or wrap individually in tissue paper or newspaper and spread out in a cool, *dark* place so fruit does not touch (never pack in boxes). If the harvest is too large for individual wrapping, spread out tomatoes (arranged by degree of ripeness) on flat surface such as a Ping-pong table (protect with newspapers) and cover with several layers of newspapers topped with a sheet. Shade any nearby windows. Important thing is to keep them ripening *slowly* with no light.

Above: Final, pre-frost October harvest [500 plus tomatoes] from just eight 7-foot high Better Boy VFN and Golden Boy plants [see photo, page 7]. During the summer, these "caged" plants had produced an additional 900 tomatoes used for summer eating and sharing plus a canned harvest of 32 quarts and 66 pints. Fresh tomatoes lasted until Christmas. See pages 33 and 83-86 for "how-to-do-it" information.

HARVESTING HINTS	STORAGE SAVVY

Tomatoes [continued]

container). When ready to use, put under cold water faucet and skins will come off instantly.

Harvested during October, tomatoes have lasted until late December using this method.

Turnips

Greens are at their most tender when about the size of your hand or smaller. Harvest roots in late summer. Roots should be about 2-2 1/2" in diameter and no more than 3".

Turnips may be left in ground until soil begins to freeze solid. Check quality, as turnips deteriorate quickly if left in the ground too long. For storage hints, see "Beets."

Zucchini — See "Squash — Summer"...

Key point is to check plants *regularly* as fruit forms almost overnight.

As with other summer squash, zucchini does not store well.

* * *

If you end up with a super abundance, as most gardeners do, check recipe books for the more unusual ways to prepare zucchini — including Zucchini

Bread (ideal for freezing) and Zucchini Cake. As another "Special for the Ladies," here's Mrs. Robert Sanders' favorite recipe for Zucchini Cake:

ZUCCHINI CAKE (serves 18) *

3 cups grated zucchini
3 cups sugar
3 cups flour
1 teaspoon baking soda
1/2 teaspoon salt
2 teaspoons baking powder
1-1/2 teaspoons cinnamon
1-1/2 cups oil
4 eggs

1 cup chopped nuts (or sprinkle on frosting)

Sift dry ingredients. Add eggs, oil and zucchini and, if desired, nuts. Place in 9" x 13" pan. Bake at 300° for 1-1/4 — 1-1/2 hours. Good with cream cheese frosting.

---

* This is just one of more than 275 tested recipes to be found in "Jams, Jellies and Desserts from Vegetables," a unique 100-page, spiral-bound cookbook of favorite ways for using the bounteous harvest from your vegetable garden. The recipes were gathered from the kitchens of MGCA members throughout the United States. Emphasis is on desserts. Cost is $4.20, including postage. Make check payable to "Men's Garden Clubs of America" and send to MGCA National Headquarters, 5560 Merle Hay Road, Des Moines, Iowa 50323. Also available upon request: free list of MGCA pamphlets on a variety of gardening topics.

ROBERT E. SANDERS is a professional writer, an experienced backyard gardener and a lecturer on innovative vegetable gardening. A native of Houston, Texas, he has a Bachelor of Science Degree in Journalism from the University of Houston and has completed academic requirements for a Master of Arts Degree from the University of Missouri School of Journalism. He is Sales Promotion Supervisor for a large life insurance company headquartered in Des Moines, IA.

ROBERT V. FISCHER, Publications Editor for a Des Moines industrial firm known for genetic developments in agriculture, has over 50 years of experience in vegetable gardening. Many of his sketches are of vegetables in his own garden. He is a former weekly newspaper owner/editor/publisher and daily newspaper news editor. Active as a lecturer on a variety of gardening topics, his academic training was in Engineering (Northern Iowa University, Iowa State University, University of Oklahoma and Louisiana State University).

In 1975, Sanders and Fischer received the MGCA's first Presidential Citations for their joint efforts in compiling and illustrating this book.

FROM A SINGLE SEED

Like Topsy, the book "A to Z Hints for the Vegetable Gardener" just grew.

It began as a 16-page summary of tips and hints for backyard gardeners prepared by MGCA member-writer Robert E. Sanders for distribution at several vegetable gardening seminars in Des Moines. Reception from novice and experienced gardeners alike was so enthusiastic that broader publication was planned in our official magazine, *The Gardener*.

Expansion of the text continued with emphasis on tips appropriate for all parts of the country, many of which had been featured in MGCA chapter news bulletins received in our office. With continued imput from our 10,000 busy home gardeners in over 250 chapters (see page 7) and the addition of the harvesting and storage section, "A to Z" quickly outgrew space restrictions in *The Gardener* and, with illustrations by MGCA member Robert V. Fischer, became MGCA's first book.

MGCA TAKES ROOT

The national organization of men gardeners was founded in Chicago on September 26, 1932 (Johnny Appleseed's birthday) by representatives from four Midwest men's clubs. Since its organization, the MGCA has been dedicated to teaching and sharing gardening with gardeners everywhere throughout the country. It has grown to over 10,000 members and has its permanent headquarters building in Des Moines, Ia.

The men sponsor the annual National Gardeners Conference, the Youth Gardeners of America, National Tree Appreciation Week and Johnny Appleseed Plant Conservation among its projects.

Information on how to organize a local men's club, or how to contact the nearest club, can be obtained by writing to: National Secretary, Men's Garden Clubs of America, 5560 Merle Hay Road, Des Moines, Iowa 50323.

Lyman E. Duncan
Executive Director